Talking Running

Stories, profiles and conversations with the running community

Noel Paine

Dedicated to all the amazing runners I have met over the years. Thank you for sharing your stories, your thoughts, feelings and time with me.

Talking Running

The stories within

This book is a collection of stories and profiles of runners from the running community – many not from Canada that I have had the privilege of profiling. Some I have chatted with, some talked to in person, others it was simply an email conversation. It was a privilege and an honour to share each story and to have met so many motivating and inspirational people. Amongst the profiles are a few stories from myself as well to mix things up.

I hope you enjoy reading the simple articles and profiles I have crafted over the years.

The first piece is a story from my past to kick things off – enjoy.

Everyone has a story to tell.

Noel

"But most of all I was inspired by the stirring examples of all the other runners. In some pictures they would seem like tiny dots in a mosaic, but each had a separate narrative starting a few months or a lifetime earlier and finishing that day in the New York City Marathon, the race with 37,000 stories."

— Mark Sutcliffe

Foreword

On May 24, 2009, when my wife was hours away from giving birth to our son, I made the wise choice of not participating in the Ottawa Marathon. Instead, I decided to spend a few minutes at the finish line of the race (with my cell phone in my hand, ready to respond!) to see some of the runners complete their races.

I had crossed many finish lines myself, but I'd never spent a lot of time watching others do it. I thought it would get repetitive after a few minutes. It didn't. On the contrary, as one runner after another crossed, I saw the relief, joy, satisfaction and elation on their faces. Without speaking with any of them, I could see how much the accomplishment meant to each. It reminded me of something Bart Yasso once said: In a marathon, all the runners travel the same route from the start to the finish line. But everyone has a different path to the start line.

Over the course of the past 15 years, I've been lucky enough to hear about thousands of those remarkable journeys. For so many amateur athletes, running represents so much more than just getting a bit of exercise. It's a validation, a reclamation, a transformation. Like that day I stood at the finish line, I have never tired of witnessing their dreams and accomplishments.

Like me, Noel Paine revels in both hearing ad sharing these stories, from the ordinary to the Olympian. This book is filled with the extraordinary adventures and fascinating anecdotes of dozens of athletes. But one of the stories which has inspired me is Noel's. In our periodic interviews on iRun Radio, Noel has shared some of his amazing achievements, including running 100 kilometres – and more – on a couple of his birthdays, ultramarathons on the trails of Italy and Ireland, and a rim-to-rim run through the Grand Canyon.

More importantly, Noel has demonstrated an indefatigable passion for mental health. He's been candid about his own experiences and he's shown a relentless determination to raise awareness and reduce the stigma of mental illness. Like so many others who travel the roads and trails, many of whom are profiled in his book, Noel uses running to prove something to himself and others.

I'm sure you'll enjoy reading the inspiring tales that follow. As Noel proves, every runner has a story to tell and a message to share. No two journeys are the same. And running has so many lessons that apply to life; it's more than a convenient metaphor, but a powerful teacher that you can travel great distances literally one step at a time.

– Mark Sutcliffe

Talking Running

Mark Sutcliffe

Mark is a respected Canadian writer, broadcaster and avid runner. He has written for newspaper and been on radio and television and has written four books, Why I Run, Canada's Magnificent Marathon, the children's book Big Joe and the Return of Football, and Long Road to Boston.

A passionate runner, Mark has completed more than 20 marathons and over the past 12 years has written books, columns and blogs and hosted a regular podcast and radio show about running. He currently blogs and writes columns for iRun magazine, which he founded in 2008.

When not working or running, Mark gives back to the running community as a member of the board of Run Ottawa and has personally raised almost $200,000 for United Way, the Ottawa Hospital and other important community causes and often does fundraisers where he runs.

Marks website: www.marksutcliffe.com

Stories

"The miracle isn't that I finished. The miracle is that I had the courage to start." - John Bingham

Talking Running

Whether you started running as a youngster or started running later – those first few running memories and experiences will stick with you. Everything is new, your legs and lungs will never burn like that before and your first race will imprint itself upon your brain. Whether magical, painful or just memorable – those memories only happen once.

Like life, running changes over time. You lose that foolish speed of youth, the lack of fear to bolt from the start line, the bottomless energy. You gain wisdom, experience and patience that would sometimes trade in for a faster 5k and more flexible hamstrings.

Enjoy the moment now, train for the future and look fondly upon the past. Most importantly, run on.

Running memories

A story from the past

Memories are what travel with us through life, the good, bad and the ugly. My collection of mental pictures from the past are littered with running stories. This is one of them.

The yearbook is black with gold writing on the back. It could be anyone's school yearbook. However, it is mine and like a magical memory-holder, it holds stories from my days of binders, lockers and teenage hormones.

One picture really brings back some early running memories. It is centred on a bet between two high school runners. It is about myself and my older friend Carl.

Carl

The smiling runner in the picture above is not me. They take pictures of the guy in the lead. I was the sweaty kid running a few minutes behind.

The runner is of Carl Erskine. It is a picture frozen in time from my high school days. A photo that jumped out at me as I was recently flipping through an old school yearbook.

In 1991 I was a six-foot, blonde-haired ninth grader at Musquodoboit Rural High School in Nova Scotia. I devoured any book or magazine about running and a dog-eared Hilroy scribbler served as my fanatical running diary. Carl was a few years older, set to graduate and the only other runner I knew.

The photos and high school yearbook that triggered the memory and the blog.

Talking Running

This is a story of one of my early running memories.

The photos and high school yearbook that triggered the memory and the blog.

The bet

It all started with a bet. The school had organized a 10K walkathon and I had gotten it into my 14-year old head that this was a great opportunity for a race. I challenged Carl the other runner in the school to a race I hoped I had a chance to win. Pocket money exchanged hands amid the smell of French fries and sweaty teenagers in our high school cafeteria. Twenty dollars was to go to the winner.

Carl was two years older and slightly more muscled than the skinny Grade 9 kid challenging him (me). I figured I ran and trained regularly and had a chance. I was no superstar but I'd run 10K in under 39 minutes and ran on the track team. I was hoping I had not bitten off more than I could...run.

The race

I took off like a mad man with Carl in tow. I think there may have been a few girls I was hoping to sprint by in the first kilometres and impress. The pace eventually slowed due to my inability to maintain it with my skinny grade-nine legs. The kilometres that had flown by at first ground to the pace of a mid-afternoon chemistry-class. Slow and painful.

My hopes of winning and being $20 richer died as Carl passed me and my fate seemed sealed. My legs were more rubbery than asking. I remember working hard but not being able to catch Carl.

Carl got the great photo of him running by in the yearbook. Both of us cannot remember the times we ran but we do remember the order in which we finished.

I am not sure why that memory stuck with me. Maybe it was still how new running was to me and it was one of my first real defeats.

I found Carl on Facebook and we briefly chatted about the event. I think it meant more to me. I have kept running but Carl claims bad ankles, I encourage him to try running again. Maybe there will be a rematch.

Run on memories.

The original version of this article was first published in Canadian Running magazine in April 2015.

I have now been running for over 30 years and have run everything from the 100m (in high school) to 100-kilometre trail ultramarathons. Running has accompanied me through life.

Running is a relatively simple sport where all you really need are shorts and shoes – and sometimes just shoes for some folks. I have always needed shoes and each running shoe is a new experience. There are many types of feet, many lengths and widths and these feet are attached to all different kinds of runners. There is no one shoe for everyone.

But when you do find that shoe that works for you, its feels right, just enough cushion, comfortable and like a part of your foot. That shoe allows you to run across the ground like the Olympic runner you dream of being.

"No doubt a brain and some shoes are essential for marathon success, although if it comes down to a choice, pick the shoes. More people finish marathons with no brains than with no shoes." - Don Kardong

Kenyan shoe company is bringing change to the nation

Kenya has established itself as the running mecca of the world. This year (2017), one running duo has launched their shoe brand- Enda- to make the country's running credentials benefit more than just their reputation.

It's no secret that Kenyans have dominated the track and the roads for many years now. These athletes are known as some of the fastest runners in the world. In fact, in 2012, Kenya had 340 runners make the qualifying time for the Olympic marathon. Now the country that produces gold medalists and world records has a new company that's creating new running shoes, developed and tested by Kenyan runners.

Called Enda, this new company's title means "Go" in Swahili. Its founders say it's meant to bring Kenyan greatness to runners around the world, and, importantly, to bring sustainable income to Kenya. Enda was founded in 2015 by Navalayo Osembo-Ombati and Weldon Kennedy.

Osembo-Ombati comes from a village near Eldoret, (a Kenyan running mecca) is an accountant and lawyer and avid runner. The two met in 2015 and started talking running when a plan was hatched. The idea was to have Kenya's running culture be of benefit to more than just its reputation. The company was created and now, they are moving from being a small start-up to selling shoes online. The first production is set to ship in April.

According to Kennedy, any elite runners were included in the testing process and provided their feedback. These included Justin Lagat and Joan Cherop Massah, among others who put thousands of kilometres in wearing their prototypes. We got a chance to talk to the creators of this up-and-coming footwear company to learn more about their future direction.

What sets these shoes apart?

Enda: *Beyond the technical aspects, we designed it to be a good looking shoe that you can wear with jeans or to brunch with mates. Of course, it's important that we're making our shoes in Kenya, the home of champions. By doing this, we're backing social impact into our shoes. When you buy an Enda shoe, you're helping create jobs in Kenya and develop a country that for decades has been famous for producing the world's best runners, but hasn't yet produced a world class running shoe.*

So why are you guys different from the many running shoe companies out there?

Enda: *The Iten is a distinct shoe from anything else out there on the market. It's designed specifically to be a lightweight trainer, that's flexible and moves with your foot. I've run in pretty much every shoe on the market that is similar to this one and I can genuinely say that the Iten makes for a more enjoyable run. We're also excited to get them to runners in a new way. By selling directly to customers online, we're able to keep the price competitive and offer runners the same shoes on a consistent basis – only making technical upgrades so as not to interfere with a runner sticking with their favourite shoe year after year.*

What do you want people to feel when they slip on a pair of your shoes?

Enda: *We hope that people feel comfortable, fast, and stylish. It's got a snug fit, so it feels almost sock-like. It's light and has a great feeling at toe-off with good ground feel, so* hopefully people also feel nice and quick in them too.

Will everyday Kenyan runners be able to wear them?

Enda: *We've actually already had a significant portion of our pre-orders from Kenya, so certainly there will already be plenty of non-professional runners here wearing them too.*

What do you hope the future holds for the company?

Enda: *We're starting with just a single excellent shoe, but we realize it's not for every runner for every run. We really want to have a full diverse product line including a more cushioned trainer, racing flat, and trail shoe. As we start to get this full range of shoes on the feet of runners around the world, we hope we can help them all find more joy and perhaps speed in their runs. If we can achieve that, it will mean bringing large amounts of revenue back into Kenya to create jobs and give back to communities. By directly connecting tens of thousands of runners around the world with Kenya, we hope to help the world better understand Kenya and Kenyan running.*

First published in Canadian Running magazine in September 2017.

Enda launched their shoes in 2017 and are continuing to make red, green and black running shoes from the land of runners. Kenyan runners continue to dominate distance running. In 2012 Kenya had to choose 3 runners for the Olympics from 300 runners who had achieved an A standard for the Games. In 2018 Kenyan Eliud Kipchoge ran 2:01:39 at the Berlin Marathon to break the world marathon record.

Running can be enjoyable and even fun but most runners have also tasted the pain that can come with it. Pushing one's boundaries can bring you to the edge of capacity, endurance and mental ability to hang on. The searing pain of a 400m race, the oxygen debt of 800m or the mile and the mental and physical battle that is the marathon. Pain is part of running especially when one challenges themselves.

"To keep from decaying, to be a winner, the athlete must accept pain--not only accept it, but look for it, live with it, learn not to fear it." - Dr. George Sheehan

Norwegian Pain Train

The relentless spin and blur of the treadmill belt is mesmerizing and annoying at the same time. It is a constant game of catch up with a motor-driven running taskmaster. I have spent countless hours on treadmills when the weather gets cold (feels like 11-months of it up here in Canada) or simply to get help forcing my body into a speed or race-pace workout. It can be a quiet struggle with just your mind and the machine.

It can also be quiet on winter ski trails, with only the sound of waxed skis on cold snow. Norway nowadays is better known for its snow and cross-country skiers like the amazing Bjørn Dæhlie than it is running, but they do have runners, and some amazing ones. Runners like the young Jakob Ingebrigtsen (and his brothers) have more recently shone light on Norway's running talent, and another Bjorn is doing the same in the ultra-running world. A news piece came up about someone setting a treadmill running record and I had to find out more.

Bjørn Tore Kronen Taranger

Bjørn is a 39-year old runner from Bergen in Norway who has a taste for pain. He is an 8-time Norwegian Champion in ultra-running with 5 titles in 24-hour running and 3 titles in the 100-klometre event. In 2017, he was 10th place at the 24-hour World Championships in Belfast, Ireland. In 2018 he was 7th at the European 24-hour Championships in Timisoara, Romania. He is also a drummer and rock band member.

In October 2018, Bjørn stepped onto a treadmill with the intent to run for 24-hours straight to raise money for kids at the Haukeland University Hospital in Bergen, Norway and to attempt to break the Guinness World Record for furthest distance run on a treadmill in 24 hours by a male (the record being 261.18km).

In an email to Runner's World Magazine, Bjørn laid out why he ran, *"I wanted to do it for all the kids that cannot walk, have heart failure, cancer, and more—for all the kids that cannot do what I can."*

Friends and family came out to support Bjørn, and celebrities ran alongside him in shifts throughout the run. He said he set the treadmill to 6.9mph and left it there and just kept running. He is someone who says he loves pain, well that is a long pain train!

Fueled by cheese pizza and snacks like salty ham, salty candy, tomatoes and drinking Coca-Cola, while staying motivated by listening to rock music, the Norwegian runner was successful.

Bjørn Tarangerto stopped the treadmill after a full day of running having raised $12,000 and having set a new world record of 264.52-kilometres.

I tracked down the record-setting ultra-runner to chat.

What made you decide to go after such a crazy treadmill record?

"First of all I wanted to raise money for all the kids at our main hospital her in Bergen (Haukeland sykehus) through the organization: «Haukelands venner». We managed to raise more than 100,000 NOK (12300 dollars ++)!! And I also

wanted to break the Guinness World Record for all the kids that can not walk, have heart failure, cancer or other things. For all the kids that can't do what I can. My passion is ultrarunning. Thats when I feel alive. And I really felt alive doing this crazy treadmill event."

How did you stay motivated and sane during the 24-hour run?

"I stayed motivated thinking of everybody that was going to get something back from what I was doing... people were very happy and inspired seeing me running on the treadmill. I stayed sane be getting my carbs and nutrition in. The best part was all the people who came to run with me, cheering with me and of course the fundraising itself. Tthe last hour was totally insane! What an epic hour, with people cheering and going crazy everywhere. It is hard to even describe the feeling. It was fucking madness."

What drives you to challenge yourself?

"I love pain! Most of all, ultrarunning is my passion. I love running and want to do it forever. I also have a big goal: I'm aiming for the World Championships title in 24 hours Running 2019!"

What has running taught you over the years?

"It has taught me a lot. I was 107,5 kg back in 2007, where I wanted to change my Rock n roll life. I played in a rock band called Goldenboy. We traveled over from Norway to USA and toured 26 states playing concerts everywhere. Running has

been life changing for me, literally! I'm at a better place physically now of course as well. I cannot see a life without running."

How would you explain ultrarunning to someone? What is the difference between a marathon and ultra for you?

"Ultrarunning is every distance from marathon and up to whatever. Some say that ultra starts from 50 km, I agree. For me a marathon is a sprint distance. Ultra is more badass! More badass to the bone. You have to be mentally stronger, especially if you do a 24 hour race."

Any future challenges or record attempts in your future?

"The next challenge will be the Bislett 24 hour indoor challenge in Oslo in the end of November 2018! No more record attempts in 2018!"

The Northern pain train may have slowed for a brief stop but sounds like it has no intention of stopping. Many runner speak of a runner high or just that healthy addiction that keeps them lacing up. It exists.

Bjørn runs with BFG Bergen løpeklubb running club in Norway and he can be found on his website and blog and on Facebook.

Bjørn's personal bests:

24-Hours	257.6km
24-Hours (treadmill)	264.52km
100-Kilometres	7:07:39
12-Hours	139 km
6-Hours	85.9 km
Marathon	2:38.31
Half-marathon	1:13:35
10-Kilometres	33:19
5-Kilometres	15:42

The mental aspect of racing and running is often as important as the physical part. Often when there is a group of elites at the start line of a big race and everyone is equally fit and no one is tremendously faster than anyone else – it's the runner who is strongest and toughest mentally who crosses the finish line first.

There is mental toughness for racing and then there is the affect running has on those who run as well. Runners often finish a run feeling calmer; less stressed out and feel better about themselves in general.

A runner, a person is more than just the pure physical form but is controlled by the thoughts and thinking inside the brain, – the mental part.

"Running is 80 percent mental." - Joan Benoit

How one documentary explores the benefits of running for those struggling with mental health

In life and running, the mental part of things is often just as important as physical health and strength. To race well and to be successful in life we need to be mentally healthy and strong.

A group behind a new running documentary: RxRun are attempting to show how running can have a positive impact on those dealing with mental health issues. This is a topic that hits close to home for me as I have battled depression and mental health and shared my journey with others. I wanted to find out more.

The film, called Rx Run, is a feature-length documentary about the positive relationship between running and mental health, seen through the lives of three teenagers that have been diagnosed with severe depression and anxiety.

The running program operates out of Credit Valley Hospital in Toronto where young people ages 15 to 24 who have battling mental illness are encouraged to join a running regimen that ends with a community 5K event. The programs started in February and ends in May with the Rx Run documentary following them on their journey.

The team consists of Bruce Baklarian, Felipe Belalcazar and Carlotta James. Baklarian and James were available to answer a few questions about their film.

Once your film is done, what do you hope people take away from it?

James: Mental health is part of who we are as human beings. We are also affected by mental health issues differently, and as such, we need different approaches to manage mental health challenges. Our documentary offers insight into one approach: to join a run therapy program.

I hope that our documentary creates greater awareness around mental health, offers solidarity to those struggling with mental health illnesses, and creates space for real dialogue to take place. Ultimately, I hope that one day we can move beyond the mainstream reliance of a pharmaceutical-

Talking Running

dominated healthcare in Canada and into one that supports a more holistic approach to dealing with mental health challenges.

Baklarian: I want the audience to understand the parallels between the progress from not being able to run much at all and feeling hopeless and depressed, to being able to run a considerable distance such as 5K or 10K and changing one's outlook on life to a more positive space.

Do you yourself run and how has that been to be involved in this project?

James: I've been running my whole life. It has been a form of medicine and meditation for me. At the end of my runs, I feel like I can take on the world and any problems that I'm faced with. For me, running is a spiritual experience, and an opportunity to connect and reconnect with nature. I also dealt with mental health issues when I was a teen as a result of living with a dysfunctional family. Running helped me deal with depression and anxiety at that time. Working on this film reminds me of the things I went through when I was a teenager, and that having strong support systems in place can make all the difference.

Baklarian: Yes, I'm a long distance runner. Running is an integral part of my life, it not only keeps me grounded and mentally in check, but it keeps me strong. I have only completed one marathon but I hope I can do a few more in my life. Since I started working on this project I have found it incredible to witness first-hand how running can be used in *such a transformative manner, especially in the lives of such an important group of people.*

First published in Canadian Running magazine in April 2017.

The RxRun documentary is 41-minutes long and is available on iTunes, Google Play and Amazon Prime. It was selected for the 2018 Buenos Aires Running Film Festival.

Ultramarathoners push themselves beyond the marathon distance where most runners stop. They push their bodies and minds to places of discomfort and discovery.

For many the finish line is 26.2 miles and that is enough struggle. Others find where the marathon ends is just the beginning and go far beyond, hours and even days more. The human body and the endurance it is capable of, is amazing.

"Run when you can, walk if you have to, crawl if you must; just never give up." - Dean Karnazes

Talking with ultramarathon runner Dean Karnazes

His website is called "ultramarathon man." Dean Karnazes is not a superhero, but he is one of the world's best ultra-marathon runners. He has run feats of endurance such as running a marathon in all 50 U.S. states in 50 days; he has won the brutal 135-mile Badwater Ultramarathon; run 350-miles in 80 hours without sleep; won numerous ultramarathon races and he has collected many awards and honours along the way.

What many may not know about the runner is that he also likes to put pen to paper to write about his running career. He has shared his adventures with readers in his books called, Ultramarathon Man: Confessions of an All Night Runner and Run! His willingness to share with the general public about going beyond 26.2 miles, in an easy to read, fun way that has gained him popularity and recognition.

Dean continues to run and write and has recently published a new book called, The Road to Sparta – reliving the ancient battle and epic run that inspired the world's greatest footrace. Dean talks about about his past and his Greek ancestry that eventually sends him off to his ancestor's country. The book tells of reconnecting with a family, an ancestry and the origins of the legendary marathon and the story and people that inspired the myth.

For so many years, so many people have told of the story of myth that lead to the idea and start of marathon races. A myth of a Greek runner named Pheidippides running 26 miles in 490 B.C. from Marathon to Athens to tell of how the Athenian army defeated the invading Persian army in a battle. The legend then says that Pheidippides makes the run, delivers his messages and then dies from the exhaustion.

I connected with Dean and asked him about his running, the book you will have to read for yourself.

What is it that drives you to run and push yourself? Why do you run?

Running is the ultimate expression of human freedom. It makes me feel alive and connects me with who I am and what I am. I strive to be the best animal that I can be and to unlock my full potential.

Did you ever think running would take you to where and what you do now?

Never could I have imagined running would take me to where I'm at today. It has been a completely unexpected journey, and a beautiful one. And quite remarkably, I still love to run as much today as the day I first began.

What was the most memorable running moment for you to this point?

When it comes to my most memorable moment in running and in life, the answer might surprise you. I've had the great privilege of running and racing on all seven continents of the planet and in some of the most remote and exotic locations on earth. I would say though that my most cherished accomplishment is running a 10-kilometer race with my daughter, Alexandria, on her 10th birthday. Nothing will ever surpass that experience.

After all you have done, are there any running adventures out there left for you?

I'm planning to embark upon a global expedition to run a marathon in every country of the world in a one-year time span. There are 203 countries and I'm working with the U.S. State Department and UN to get the necessary passports and permits to be able to do this. As you can imagine, the planning, logistics and sponsorship negotiations are every bit as complex and difficult as the running itself. But I like the challenge of all these elements. I'm inviting the local country people to come run with me when I'm visiting. It might be naive of me, but I think humanity could use something like this right now. Let's stop fighting with each other and start running together. This is my small contribution to the world I love.

First published in Canadian Running magazine in February 2017.

Dean is always running and keeping busy. He now has his own wine made from grapes from Greece and is showcasing his documentary 'Road to Sparta' about his run at the famous Spartathlon ultramarathon.

Some more about Dean's running and feats of endurance:

- Ran 350 miles (560 km) in 80 hours and 44 minutes without sleep in 2005.
- Has completed "The Relay", a 199-mile (320 km) run from Calistoga to Santa Cruz, 11-times.
- Ran a marathon to the South Pole in 2002
- Ran a marathon in each of the 50 states in 50 consecutive days in 2006.
- Winner, Badwater Ultramarathon in 2004 (with five other top-10 finishes from 2000-2008).
- Winner, Vermont Trail 100 Mile Endurance Run, 2006.
- Overall Winner, 4 Deserts Race Series, 2008.
- American Ultrarunning Team, World Championships, 2005, 2008.
- 148 miles (238 km) in 24 hours on a treadmill, 2004.
- Eleven-time 100-Mile/1 Day Silver Buckle holder at the Western States Endurance Run, 1995–2006.
- Ran 3,000 miles (4,800 km) across the United States from Disneyland to New York City in 75 days in 2011.
- Has across the San Francisco Bay

Running itself produces endorphins that are like natural painkillers. A drug. Many runners can come across as addicted. Some runners may push running to an unhealthy level that affects their work and personal life. There is always someone who goes too far.

But – there are worse addictions. This is when sometimes, running can be the drug that helps. Running is never the solution buts seems to help some find a healthier, happier way to live.

"The point is whether or not I improved over yesterday. In long-distance running the only opponent you have to beat is yourself, the way you used to be." - Haruki Murakami

Running Helps Runner Recover

A former addict finds more than sweat and fitness from running.

It's the holiday season and a time of hope. This seems like a good time for a running story that fits right into the season as well. Barry is a runner from Ottawa, who not that long ago, probably would never have imagined that he might be able to run a half-marathon. Most of Barry's goals were simple and short term: where and how to get drugs and repeat.

Barry

Head down and mind solely on the task of running Barry runs the inaugural Ottawa Mission Possible Half Marathon in November 2011. Photo: Doug Sasaki.

For eight hard years, Barry was fueled by crack. Crack was Barry's evil master that once gripped his shoulders, watched him go for 17 days straight and drained him until he weighed only 135 pounds. Barry's addiction cost him a good job and a house, but it hasn't yet won.

Finding Running

I found running as a youngster was something that let me get a handle on a bad temper that was leading me into bigger and bigger holes I was having trouble climbing out of. Running allowed me to learn patience, perseverance and kept me on an even keel emotionally. Running has accompanied me through the good and bad times of life. I'm thankful that I

Talking Running

found the sport. I was interested to hear what Barry thought of running.

Barry is 44 and discovered running in July when he joined a five-month addiction treatment program run by the Ottawa Mission. This was not Barry's first attempt at getting clean but this was another real attempt to turn his life around. The Mission also had a running group that met on Saturdays. It wasn't a big group and for many, it was a walk, not a run. For some reason, Barry chose to try running.

The first race

To keep this blog to a reasonable length and to allow me to share some of Barry's words and thoughts I will jump ahead. In November, Barry lined up for a half-marathon organized by the Running Room just outside Ottawa. Exceeding all expectations Barry ran his first half-marathon in 1:37. His name was mentioned in a newspaper article. Barry and I made contact and I asked him about his story and his running.

Why did running interest you?

I arrived in Ottawa, July 16, 2011 in pretty rough shape emotionally, spiritually, and physically. I hadn't any idea what was before me but knew I needed help and was willing to make big changes in my life. Once I was settled in at Ottawa Mission's 'Lifehouse,' someone told me about the Mission's running program and decided to give it a try. I had quit smoking cigarettes the week before so my first run on

July 30th was a 5K walk/run. Needless to say I could have never imagined that I would be running in a half marathon three and a half months later.

Why did you keep running?

At first I enjoyed the camaraderie and new friendships that came with participating in the running program. I would run with Chris and Roberto every Saturday morning and they would encourage me to 'ramp up' and concentrate on proper form. I also had a running buddy that was in the Mission's 'Stabilization' wing and we ran together but such is with the nature of addiction he left and I found myself having to run alone if I wanted to continue. I donned my MP3 player and found a reprieve from everyday stress. I noticed that I was much less anxious, my mood was more stable, and I my self-esteem increased. I recognized the benefits immediately.

How has running changed you?

Running has given me the ability to dream and set goals again. With Chris and Roberto's coaching, they helped me achieve a goal I never thought possible. Today I know that as long as I keep my recovery first and do the work, I can achieve almost anything. I am much more easy going and my mind doesn't race like it used too.

After your first race, what are your goals now?

My number one goal is to stay clean obviously. I have committed to stay in Ottawa for at least one year. I really love this city and all its beauty. I intend to join "The Running

Room" Sunday morning run as the Missions running program has shut down for the winter. I am going to run the Ottawa Race Week-end half-marathon on the May 24th weekend. I am also considering the Army Run and a race in Montreal. I still run about five days a week and enjoy every minute of it. Winter running brings on new challenges but I think it just makes us runners tougher and stronger!

What would you say to others struggling with an addiction or problem, how does running help?

Ultimately everyone's struggles and journey is unique. I encourage anyone who may be in the disease of addiction, dealing with depression or what have you, to give running a try. Reach out to a group like I did. If it turns out running is not your thing, find something that you can be passionate about. To quote Winston Churchill "Never, ever, ever, ever, ever, ever, ever, give in. Never give in. Never give in. Never give in." Happy running everyone!

Barry says he is not a crack-addict. One is never the drug or addiction that owns them, they are a person dealing with something that has gotten out of control. Barry is now a runner, a label that doesn't need removing and may lead him down roads he never thought possible.

I ran with Barry a few weeks before the holidays and I think that half-marathon PB will be destroyed in May.

See you on the roads Barry, we are all cheering for you, welcome to the Canadian running family.

Talking Running

This article was originally published in Canadian Running magazine in December 2011. I have not used Barry's photo as I cannot get hold of him – and not sure if he is still running – I hope he is.

Running is never the solution but myself and many other shave found running can help with stress and mental health issues. Many well-known runners like ultramarathoner Charlie Engle (Book: Running Man) have written about how running has helped them with addiction.

There are different types of runners. There are those who take up running later in life, to battle the bulge or to get in to better shape. There are those who run in high school and then never after, but will always talk about their running years. There are those who simply find a love for lacing up at random somewhere in life.

Then there a few who latch onto running early on, who are either gifted runners or simply are drawn to the sport like a magnet. They may like to race but it is the act of running they are drawn to, and they become lifelong runners.

"Every morning in Africa, a gazelle wakes up, it knows it must outrun the fastest lion or it will be killed. Every morning in Africa, a lion wakes up. It knows it must run faster than the slowest gazelle, or it will starve. It doesn't matter whether you're the lion or a gazelle – when the sun comes up, you'd better be running." - Christopher McDougall

Elana Meyer: A South African blast from the past

"My best days still start with a run in the mountains – I run for good health, energy, and to clear my head!" — Elana Meyer

If you remember such things as telephones that had cords, televisions that weighed as much as small cars and race t-shirts that were cotton, then you are probably around my age. I have now survived four decades on this beautiful earth. When I was a young impressionable (and skinny) young runner, I sought out anything to do with running, in book form or on the television just the way kids nowadays seek out... well I'm not too sure.

One of the runners who I watched glide across the behemoth box of a television screen in my Nova Scotia childhood home and who graced the pages of magazines was a runner by the name of Elana Meyer. For those who need help remembering, she ran at the same time as those like Zola Budd and Mary Decker Slaney, other elites on the world stage.

She ran like the wind and she and many others from that era and the past are the ones who fueled my running dreams. They lit that fire, the desire to try to run like them. It's one that still burns.

I recently had the chance to ask one of my childhood running heroes a few questions.

But first, a bit about her.

Elana Meyer

Elana Meyer is an Olympic distance runner from South Africa, who among other things, won silver in the 10,000m at the 1992 Summer Olympics. I remember her lean physique and her short-cropped brown hair and her smooth stride.

Running in South Africa, Meyer won her first half-marathon in 1980 at the age of 13. She ran 1:27. Meyer grew up on her family's farm and was the second of four children. It was not long until she was competing against another soon-to-be famous South African runner, the barefoot running Zola Budd. Meyer worked hard and began to gain success. Unable to compete on the world stage for many years during the country's Apartheid, it was not really until 1992 when Meyer got to shine.

In 1992, Meyer ran to a silver medal in the 10,000m at the summer Olympics. She is also remembered for embracing and running a victory lap with the Ethiopian winner, to thunderous applause.

Talking Running

Aside from her Olympic medal, she also set African records in the 15K and the half-marathon, was the gold medalist in the half-marathon at the 1994 World Championships and set world records at that distance four times. She retired from competition in 2005.

After some email correspondence, Meyer and I connected and I got the chance to ask a few simple questions.

Looking back on your running career and running in general, what has it done for you?

Running gave me an amazing opportunity to create a life through sport. I made a career out of my sport and travelled the world. I met amazing people and experienced great highlights. Today I am still involved with the sport — giving a next generation a chance to develop. I still try to run every day. Running still energizes me, it keeps me healthy and fit, it clears my head (cheap psychology).

What drives you to keep running and what is the motivation now?

My best days still start with a run in the mountains. I run for good health, energy, and to clear my head!

Any running goals for the rest of 2015 or long term?

I have done some marathons as charity runs with people but have not raced since I retired in 2005. I did an eight-day mountain bike stage race, Cape Epic, which was a great challenge which I loved. I will be turning 50 next year and I would still like to do an Ironman and run a stage trail race but my biggest satisfaction comes from the goals of doing successfully what I have set out to do: seeing young runners improve at Cape Town Marathon, Endurocad.

Meyer is currently co-director of the South African Endurance Academy, a non-profit organization that provides a complete sports management solution for aspiring endurance athletes. She is also involved with the Cape Town Marathon which she hopes to help make into the country's biggest race.

Having the chance to talk with her was an honour and made me think of my early days of as a young runner. It's often that our childhood heroes star in our dreams and set fire to our desires.

First published in Canadian Running magazine in December 2015.

A little more about Elana:

She has set 23 South African records and near the end of 2001, in her very first race as a veteran (the veteran age limit set by Athletics South Africa is 35), established her first world age 35-39 record when she clocked an SA senior 10 km record of 31:13 in Budapest.

Personal bests:

1500m   4:02.15

3000m	8:32.00
5000m	14:44.05
10,000m	30:52.51
5K	15:10
10K	31:13
Half	1:06.44
Marathon	2:25.15

Running connects people. It is one of the few sports where the elites, the mid-packers and even those who are just hoping to finish, can all line up together. Big egos are rare and runners tend to be humble and friendly. There is a respect for each other and a comradery.

Most runners wave when passing a fellow runner, even from the other side of the street. Sometimes we wonder what their story is, what they are training for – then you continue your run.

"If you are losing faith in human nature, go out and watch a marathon." - Kathrine Switzer

Runner at the corner

There are points in your life when something might make you stop and think, maybe even make you smile. Maybe something jostles loose a train of thoughts. One day, on a corner not long ago, I ran into a runner who made me think and smile.

Winter traffic light. I looked over at the intersection. He was tall and even through his baggy jeans and thin winter jacket I could detect a lean body. I guessed he was in his late twenties or early thirties. Dark eyes, a lean face and dark skin peered out from the space left between tuque and a scarf wrapped around his face. Something about him said runner.

It was my regular run home. It was a workout day, I'd finished a hard treadmill session at noon but had some energy left, some juice left in the legs for the scamper home. Now, I wasn't setting any land speed records, but was probably with pack and all running pretty quickly.

The corner or intersection was a regular stop for me. Unless I arrived perfectly on time, I had to wait for cars to turn, see the white walk signal and boot it up a long solid hill. It was only a couple kilometres from home, so, if I felt fresh, I could always push it without worry of dragging my sorry self the rest of the way. I usually stood alone on that corner while watching cars roll past. I rarely met too many runners going the same way. I had stopped at the corner and not noticed the company of another until I looked over. This day, the tall stranger was dressed for a winter walk home. He was bundled up with a winter jacket, winter hiking-style boots and jeans. He looked over, for some reason I sensed a kinship and nodded.

I darted when the lights turned and headed through the intersection, foot on the sidewalk and started pumping up the hill. My legs felt good and I pushed off lightly with each foot. I tried to stay smooth. Maybe I was impressing the tall walker behind me. The hill was about 300 metres long. I stayed strong and eased off a bit as I hit the top and ran across the next intersection at the top of the hill just as the light was turning. For some reason I glanced back.

Just as I hit the other side I caught a glimpse of my walking friend at the crest of the hill, at the intersection I'd just crossed. I stopped, stunned. I turned to face him and we exchanged a smile. I laughed and pointed in the direction I was running over the cars between us. He pointed in the opposite direction.

Something said this guy was a runner. He'd felt the challenge of camaraderie with another runner. I should have run after, or in his direction to find out his story. Boots and all, he'd chased me unheard up that hill, and smiled after. Was he a Kenyan? Was my runner at the corner some Kenyan come to Canada - longing to stretch out his legs and run? Was he just a guy having fun? Who knows? The runner on the corner. For me a story untold.

Originally published in Canadian Running magazine in March 2014.

Racing on foot is so much more than one foot in front of the other and aiming for a certain time. There is the physical training, the hours spent sweating and the many miles covered usually alone, but that is often not enough. Racing is not just physical but mental. So often the person who has more guts or grit can out race someone sometimes who is fitter.

Racing is very often not a race against those around you but a battle with yourself. Its about fighting the pain, the discomfort and being able to push beyond the comfortable long enough to get your goal or pass that other runner.

"A lot of people say they love running because of how they feel afterward. Not me. Well, I love that, too, but it's also so much fun while I'm out there." - Dick Beardsley

Talking with American marathon legend Dick Beardsley

Dick Beardsley is one of the United States' most notable distance runners in part because of his 1982 Boston Marathon battle, dubbed "Duel in the Sun," with the now-coach Alberto Salazar.

Beardsley was 21 when he ran his first marathon, a 2:47 in Wisconsin. Following that run, his times continued to drop. Beardsley earned a spot in the Guinness Book of World Records for running 13 consecutive personal bests in the marathon.

Racing during what was a distance running boom in Canada and the United States, Beardsley ran fast times even by today's standards. His 2:09:37 at the 1981 Grandma's Marathon stood as a course record for 33 years.

Beardsley finished second behind Salazar, currently the coach of the Nike Oregon Project and Canadian Cam Levins, at the 1982 Boston Marathon and his time was under the previous American and Boston course records. His second-place time of 2:08:53 would be his finest-ever performance and is written about in detail in Duel in the Sun.

In 2010, Beardsley was inducted into the U.S. National Distance Running Hall of Fame.

Dick Beardsley

Now living in Bemidji, Minn. he owns and runs a bed and breakfast, operates his own fishing guide business and continues to find the time to do motivational speaking.

I reached out to Beardsley and had the chance to ask one of U.S. running's biggest names a few questions.

What drives you to continue to be involved with the running community?

"Even though I'm now slower than molasses in January compared to my younger days I still go to bed at night and can hardly wait to get up to go for a run. I've been running for almost 44 years and love it as much as ever. I also do

some online coaching and I get such a thrill from helping other runners reach their goals."

How often do you run these days?

"I run every day and most of it is at a pretty slow pace. I run about 50 miles (80K) per week now. I really don't have anything that motivates me to run, I just love doing it."

Everyone remembers you for the Duel in the Sun with Alberto but besides the 1982 race, what is the most memorable moment of your competitive career?

"That race is right up towards the top. The one that means the most to me though was the 1981 Grandma's Marathon in Duluth, Minn. I was fortunate to win that race with a time of 2:09:36 but it meant so much to me because my mom and dad were both at the finish line to see me win. They had never seen me run a marathon before and my dad, who you could have hit over the head with a two-by-four, was crying like a baby when I finished. I'll never forget that day."

What was the greatest struggle or battle for you in life and in running?

"The greatest battle in running was making sure I kept my training under control. It was hard for me to run easy on my easy days and hard not to run 20 miles every day. Until seven months ago I would have told you it was when I became addicted to prescription pain killers. I've been very fortunate to have 19 years of sobriety from them. I never thought anything could ever be tougher to deal with. Then this past

October my son Andy took his life. He suffered from PTSD when he got back from being deployed in Iraq while serving in the United States Army. I still find it hard to believe he is gone but I've received so much support from my wife Jill and other family and friends. I've also written a few songs about that day and my son and that has helped me cope with his death."

What advice from your running and life experiences would you pass on to others?

"Don't ever give up. There are four things I try and do every morning when I wake up. Over the years, through my speaking, I've passed it onto others hoping that these four things help them: When I wake in the morning I try and have a smile on my face, enthusiasm in my voice, joy in my heart and faith in my soul."

This article was originally published in Canadian Running magazine in May 2016.

A little more about Dick Beardsley:

- Inducted into the National Distance Running Hall of Fame – 2010
- 2009 The Running Event Hall of Fame & Lifetime Achievement Award Winner.

- Two-time champion, 1981 & 1982 - Grandma's Marathon
- Course record holder (2:09:37) - 1981 Grandma's Marathon
- Champion and course record holder (2:16:20) - 1987 Napa Valley Marathon
- 1981 London Marathon champion (2:11:48)
- Second-place finish - "The Duel in the Sun" - Boston 1982 - (2:08:53)
- Two-time Olympic Trials Marathon qualifier - 1980 & 1988
- Guinness Book of World Records - Only man to have ever run 13 consecutive personal bests in the marathon
- Road Runners Club of America Hall of Fame - inducted 1989
- American record holder for 10 miles on the track 49:05 – 1982
- 2006 and 2007 RRCA National Masters Marathon Champion

Runners are so often humble because there is always someone faster. Running is a solo pursuit, even when training with a group. When running, training or racing it is a battle of mind and body to push to your best.

One's best is most often determined by genetics and factors such as biomechanics, V02max and ability to handle training. There are some things that can be improved and then some that we have no control over. It can be humbling. We all train to see improvement and to reach a goal, its personal and individual.

"Mental will is a muscle that needs exercise, just like the muscles of the body." – Lynn Jennings

Talking Running

Catching up with Trevor Hofbauer

In late fall/ early winter, many are looking back on what they achieved this season. On a fall day in Philadelphia not long ago, one Canadian runner itching to make it to the world stage ran across the finish line of the 2015 Philadelphia Marathon with a time of 1:04:28. It was a personal best and a time that meets the Canadian standard (1:06) for an athlete to run at the world half-marathon championships. Trevor Hofbauer was so fast that he hammered through the 10K mark in a personal best time (30:19).

I got a second to ask the newly-mustached Calgary area runner a few questions.

How did it feel crossing the line in Philadelphia with a world champ qualifying time?

Honestly, words can't express how satisfied I was to cross that line. In a single moment, the training, the sacrifices, the dedication– it all payed off. It has been a dream of mine to represent Canada on the world stage. Now that might become a reality.

Did the mustache make you faster?

Yes, absolutely! This mustache may not be the world's best mustache, but the grouping of 12 hairs above my lip shows commitment, dedication, and persistence. It keeps the ladies away, allowing me to live distraction free and it reminds me that there's work to do. This mustache also boosts my mental strength attributes by three points.

Now that Philly is over and you have achieved this goal, what is the plan?

The smart thing to do right now is rest. This year has been busy with work, travel, and athletics, so I'm thinking of getting back in the groove soon.

My current plan is to run a 10K before March, then hopefully I'll get the call on March 10th. All of my focus is on Cardiff. It's going to be tough training for a race that isn't guaranteed, but I'm prepared for booth scenarios (getting or not getting the call) and will play it by day.

What are your long term running goals as a runner?

As a runner, my long term goal is to represent Canada at the 2020 & 2024 Olympics for the marathon. I have a few side *goals to that but if I can get a little bit better every day, those long term goals will be attainable. Ultimately, my long term goal is to be a positive role model within the running community. Being a part of the community gives me a different perspective on the sport, it allows me to remain level-headed and I'm able to meet so many people with amazing stories. This sport is a gift; that's how I perceive it. At the end of the day, I want to be known as the kid with a ton of heart before I'm labelled as the kid with fast legs."*

What drives you to run (and race) and keeps you motivated?

My drive comes from seeing constant improvement and knowing that there are others who look up to me. When I first started out running, the Calgary running community really welcomed me. From there, I started running with the Bow Valley Harriers/MitoCanada crew. Runners like Jeremy Deere, Blaine Penny, Lisa Harvey, Adam Kahtava, and Dave Proctor showed me the way by sharing their own stories and accomplishments. A lot of my drive and motivation comes from the inspirational stories of Blaine Penny and Dave Proctor. I wouldn't be able to do what I do without the ongoing support of the Calgary running community. That keeps me motivated."

First published in Canadian Running magazine in December 2015.

Trevor has continued to train and race since I profiled him in 2015. In 2016 he was third at the Canadian XC

Championship (10k) in 29:56 and was third Canadian at the famous Vancouver Sun Run 10k in 29:28. In 2017 in won the Athletics Ontario XC Championship (10k) in 32:23 was the top Canadian at the Toronto Waterfront Marathon in 2:18:05 and represented Canada at the IAAF World XC Championship and NACAC XC Championship. In 2018 in addition to a number of road race wins Trevor was the Canadian National Half Marathon Champs with a time of 1:08:26.

Personal bests:

Marathon: 2:18:05	Toronto Marathon, 2017
Half Marathon: 1:04:28	Philadelphia Marathon, 2015
10K (Road): 29:24	Eastside 10K, 2018
8K (Road): 23:33	NACAC XC Champs, 2017
5K (Road): 14:33	Yorkville 5K , 2016

Running has so often been a place where race, religion, skin colour and sex make no difference. We all line up at the same line. It has not always been this way and women have had to fight to run distance races and racism and other issues arise – but it can be a place of equality.

On the road, track or trail, we are all just runners, united by a love of running and all running towards the same finish line.

"We can only see a short distance ahead, but we can see plenty there that needs to be done." – Alan Turing

Talking Running

A running tale from the past and across the water

A story of more than running

The apple sits quietly on the white sill of the open window.

Alan watches it and then runs a finger down the shiny red skin that reflects the summer sun.

A is for Apple. It is supposed to be A is for Alpha in the military phonetic alphabet, but Alan had always preferred the imagery of an apple. It made him think of his favourite folk story about Snow White and the Seven Dwarves.

Working as a code breaker during the war, breaking the secrets of the German Enigma machine had earned him the Order of the British Empire. Some say it helped bring the war to an end years early. Not that he could tell anyone, he was still sworn to secrecy years later.

Alan's thoughts are drawn to the white cotton as it shifts in the early summer almost flicking at the apple. The innocent clothes moves at the bid of the moods of Mother Nature.

Talking Running

The thought of summer sun and ruffled cotton takes Alan's thoughts back to the summer of 1947.

Blessed with a gifted mind for numbers, Alan also had legs that could propel him for miles. It was like his body and mind craved it, respite from the mental turmoil, he reveled in pushing himself, minutes and miles slipping away in the joy of running. In a fight to defeat the Nazis in the war, he had run when he could find time, getting some satisfaction in beating his colleagues to meetings, often more than forty kilometres away.

Alan reveled a bit in his eccentricity, he knew he was different but at the same time ached to be allowed to fit in. A coffee cup chained to the radiator so no one would steal it, his ever-churning mind and his running; it was who he was, as much as he could reveal.

His mind was too busy for how to properly tie a Windsor knot or iron his pants and when his legs craved to run, he ran.

His mind is now quiet. His legs twitch in readiness after being tested in the previous months. Miles of training and preparation had honed his legs and body. It is August 23rd, a date he has drawn circles around in pencil on the calendar.

Other human gazelles, edgy to start, line the road around him. The race will determine who represents England in the marathon at the 1948 Olympic Games. His mind has worked out the training and what it will take to run his best, but this is a place where calculations and codes do not exist.

The starter's gun shatters the silence. Alan finds himself caught up in the melee of the anxious start. Elbows fly, legs and feet churn frantically but foolishly, grappling for spots in the first few metres of a race that will last for almost three hours.

When nerves settle, Alan finds himself at peace. His mind clicks into running mode and his body moves into a familiar marathon gear.

Alone in his own battle, doubts and the course, Alan pushes the pace and grunts as he does when running hard. He also feels a sense of freedom that running gives him.

With feet flying, any calculations are pushed aside for a moment. It is one foot after the other. He is in the the chase.

Crossing the finish line in fifth place in a time of 2:46, Alan places his hands on his knees, his chest still heaving. It is a good effort, but not being in the top three means he isn't going to the Olympics. The well-wishers weave around him to greet others. He is just another runner.

It has been two years since his last race and five years since his attempt at making the Olympic team. An injury has also pruned Alan's ability to quench the thirst for flying over turf and road on foot.

Alan no longer runs, but he's restless. He feels caught in a cage. He can see and hear, his mathematical mind still looks for a challenge but he feels lost.

The war is over. Secret work cracking codes and pushing himself to the limit is over as well.

Working in a secret building in England, he had been the one chasing, far from the guns but with the real pressure to save lives and help end a war.

Funny how he was the one that had been pursued after.

Alan Turing was a code breaker and mathematician who played a major role in bringing the Second World War to an end. He is regarded as a pioneer in modern computer science.

Turing was prosecuted in the UK for being homosexual when it was criminalized there during the 1950s. He was given hormone treatment in exchange for prison time as a sentence for being homosexual. He died in 1954 after eating an apple laced with cyanide. The death was determined to be a suicide.

First published in Canadian Running magazine in March 2014.

A little more about Alan Turing's running:

Talking Running

Alan reportedly ran a little while he was in grade school, usually when football was cancelled because of bad weather and rowed rather than ran when at Cambridge for his undergrad degree. When he studied at King's College he is said to have begun to run more seriously, his frequent route being from Cambridge to Ely and back, a distance of around 50 km.

He did a little running while doing his code-breaking at Bletchley Park but when he moved to the National Physical Laboratory he took up running more seriously. He was described as tremendously fast and a noisy runner, grunting as he flew by.

Turing came fifth in the AAA marathon which was used as a qualifying event for the 1Olympic Games. His time was 2:46:03, only 10-minutes slower than the Olympic winning time the next year in 1949.

Meditation and running do not always sound like they would go together. Running often feels like a truly physical endeavor and sometimes on tough runs it is just sweat, effort and a lot of concentration. It sometimes does not feel calming or meditative.

There are runs, maybe on the trail, where it's quiet, maybe it's a beautiful place to run and your mind goes elsewhere or it's a chance to think on things. You sometimes can come back from a run feeling refreshed and thinking clearer.

"Running and meditation are very personal activities. Therefore they are lonely. This loneliness is one of their best qualities because it strengthens our incentive to motivate ourselves." – Sakyong Mipham

Mixing Running and Meditation

Speaking with Buddhist leader and runner Sakyong Mipham meditattion and his new book about running.

In my hometown of Halifax there is a Buddhist center tucked away downtown not far from Point Pleasant Park, one of the favourite local running spots. I have been to the Buddhist Centre (Halifax Shambhala Center) and sat uncomfortably with my tight runner hamstrings screaming while trying to meditate. Not long after, as coincidence would have it, I met its leader while working at the local running shop, he was shopping for running gear; I believe as I was looking into Buddhism, he was looking into running.

I was intrigued then but only now many years later, did I get the privilege to communicate with and write about this runner and spiritual leader.

Sakyong Mipham

Sakyong Mipham is a Tibetan lama and the leader of Shambhala, a global community of meditation retreat centers (including one in Halifax) grounded in realizing basic goodness and an enlightened society through daily life. The 50-year-old, who looks younger than his years, has close-cropped hair, and a smile that always seems genuine and is also a father to a young daughter born in 2010.

He is also an avid runner who has completed 9 marathons. Sakyong Mipham teaches all over the world, using his unique blend of Eastern and Western perspectives to the benefit of his students in North and South America, Europe, and Asia. As well as being one of the world's top mediators and spiritual leader, Sakyong Mipham has a personal best of of 3:05 for the marathon, which he ran at the Chicago Marathon in 2006. Other marathons he has run include Edmonton, NYC and the famous Boston marathon.

Reaching out to the spiritual leader after my interest in him was sparked by the publication of his new book called "Running with the Mind of Meditation." I had the privilege of asking him a few questions.

When did you begin running and why?

"I began running in 2002 for a number of reasons. At first it was about getting physically stronger and connecting with the environment. Then, it started to take on more social qualities, like making personal connections with people and running for good causes."

What role has running played in your role as a spiritual leader and in your personal life?

"Since running is a big part of who I am, it naturally affects my teaching on meditation and my personal life. For me it has always been an integrated experience. When meditation came to the West, it was disembodied and dissociated from regular, daily activity. But the tradition of meditation is actually about being very present and very embodied – being engaged with what is going on personally and culturally. Disembodiment causes a lot of the stress that is prevalent in our society. But, as I say in the book, "Movement is good for the body and stillness is good for the mind." It really comes down to having a healthy relationship with your own life."

What does your book about meditation and running give insight into, and why should someone read it?

"Running with the Mind of Meditation talks about synchronizing the body and mind beginning with physical exercise. If you can bring these simple meditative principles into your daily routine, not only will your workouts be more rewarding, but your whole life will become infused with those good qualities."

What races or marathons have you completed and how do you choose where and what race you will run?

"I have completed nine marathons and one half marathon. They were all very different races, but the one thing that they all had in common was the sense of connecting with the environment and the community. No matter where we run, there is always a feeling of communicating with our surroundings and those around us. Whether we are running in a city or out in nature, we can connect in a very immediate way. At the same time, it is essential to communicate with those around us. This kind of connection and communication is a part of being alive. It inspires us and makes us stronger, allowing us to communicate with the world in much subtler ways."

My often-feeble attempts and problems with running may be tied to my lack of mental fortitude and maybe I need to not only look to train my legs but also my mind. Running can do so much good and can be used to help many overcome many challenges, but regardless of beliefs, religion or marathon times, a focused, clear and peaceful mind always comes in handy.

Run on Sakyong Mipham. Welcome to the Canadian running community when you are amongst us.

This article was originally published in Canadian Running magazine in June 2012. Sakyong continues to run and is now the father of three girls.

Running can make you feel better in body and mind. So often, things seem less complicated or you are able to see a solution you did not before your run. Therapy can be a great way to seek help, hear your own thoughts and feelings and get guidance to mental health or a happy life.

Combining running and therapy can only be a good thing right?

"I had as many doubts as anyone else. Standing on the starting line, we're all cowards." - Alberto Salazar

Runing and therapy?

A chat with the founder of Dynamic Running Therapy, an approach which combines psychotherapy, mindfulness and movement to help with mental health issues.

Running Dad

A chat about running, therapy and how the two can help mental health.

William Pullen is a 50-year old and lives in London, England but for a time lived in Toronto, Ontario. He is a psychotherapist, runner, author, and app developer and the founder of Dynamic Running Therapy (DRT). DRT is a therapy approach which combines psychotherapy, mindfulness and movement.

Along with using and promoting this new type of therapy that combines lacing up and more traditional therapy, Pullen has written a book about it called, 'Running with Mindfulness: Dynamic Running Therapy (DRT) to Improve

Low-mood, Anxiety, Stress, and Depression'. He took a moment to chat about his book and DRT.

How did the idea of the book come about – and how did the idea for DRT come to you?

"DRT first – I had a bit of a meltdown about 11 years ago. I found myself depressed, scared and anxious. I knew I had to do something to help myself so decided to go into therapy, take up running and do yoga. It was while running with a friend who was going through a divorce that I discovered how helpful it could be. We both found ourselves talking very easily – what we were feeling seemed to flow freely, as though the running somehow was giving us clarity and license.

The running also helped us to feel better on a physical level, as well as being psychologically empowering – no bad thing when you are depressed! It was a relief to have a practice whereby I could show up, talk easily and feel refreshed and strong at the end of it. Not long after that I decided to train to become a psychotherapists and over the next 6 years took what I felt was best from my training and incorporated it into what became DRT."

Who do you think can benefit from reading your book?

"Well the book contains a number of different things so is potentially attractive to all sorts of people. It has guides for mindful running and mindful walking which most people can benefit from. It also has specific programs for the treatment

of depression, anxiety, anger and relationship issues, among other things. Each program takes the reader on a journey of self-discovery and growth using a combination of walking, running, and mindfulness. I ask them to walk or run with questions which address how they relate to themselves and others, lifestyle choices, their personal background, and the choices they are making today as well as the beliefs that they hold about themselves and the world.

RUNNING
WITH
MINDFULNESS

DYNAMIC
RUNNING
THERAPY
(DRT)
TO IMPROVE
LOW-MOOD,
ANXIETY,
STRESS, AND
DEPRESSION

WILLIAM PULLEN

The book also contains programs for running with your kids, as well as something called Empathy Runs which are a great way for bonding and sharing special moments with the people in your life."

What is it about running that can help those dealing with mental health issues?

"I believe that sometimes words alone are not enough for some people, and that through applying ourselves physically to our situation we can embody the kind of change and growth we are looking for. In other words, the strength and confidence I experience from the outdoors and from becoming the person who can get from A to M and then finally to Z helps empower me and heal me. You see mental health issues and debilitating and anything you can do to empower and help focus that person is of benefit. It's a kind of hack

sometimes but it really works. Of course its hard to show up when you're depressed – really hard. But if we can make showing up feel like a rejuvenating, healing experience it becomes easier. Its also a great way to burns of energy if anxiety is an issue."

What is one simple thing runners can try?

"They could try Empathy Runs – you can find this on my website but simply put it involves: Two people running together for about 20 to 30 mins. One person listens (no interrupting, helping, saving, encouraging) in silence then repeats back a synopsis of what they have heard. Then the roles are swapped. It's an incredible way to feel heard and unburden yourself in a healthy way of some of the natural stresses we have in our life. Of course its not always about stress – sometimes they become gratitude runs.

Or they could try and bit of mindful running – this involves emptying the mind of thoughts about yesterday and tomorrow and instead concentrating on the here and now – this is done either through focusing on the breath as you run (count to 10 and start again) or every other footfall. To begin with you will find yourself getting to footfall/breath 2 or 3 or 4 and then thoughts about the future or past will creep in. At this point you acknowledge that thought, let it go, and start back at one again. The real practise is not in trying to get to 10 uninterrupted because its not about success and goals. It's about meeting your inner dialogue with whom we often have a dubious and ambivalent relationship with and trying to improve it through gentle recognition and acknowledgement f what is going on. So often we are caught up between pushing ourselves and then castigating ourselves when we don't get to where we wanted to be – this is a tough prism through which to experience the world. Mindful running helps you find a more compassionate and easy going way of being – one that is actually more productive because it wastes less energy. "

If you find running a form of therapy and stress relief already, DRT may be something you should lace up for and learn more about.

I personally really like the read and it all made sense to me. I have a background in psychology and neuroscience and have been a runner for 30-years. The book is easy to read, straight forward and has a section where you get exercises to do and space to jot down notes/thoughts. Worth finding online and ordering.

Pullen runs now for fun and to stay in shape and can be found online on his website and on Twitter @PullenTherapy.

William Pullen

* In Canada – Kristy McConnell (Alberta) combines walking, running and therapy and is a runner. Her website: https://www.obpwellness.com/

First published in May 2018 on my personal blog.

Running like life requires us to adapt to what comes up to meet us on the trail, road or track. Life throws us unexpected events and brings us changes we have to overcome.

Being adaptable, flexible, patient, calm and able to be positive when there is change and when things can get tough is a great skill to have.

"Running allows me to set my mind free. Nothing seems impossible. Nothing unattainable." — Kara Goucher

Talking Running

Talking to a running dad on Father's Day

'Becoming a father changes your life forever."

This is a blog profile of a runner who has adapted to runningdad life like I wish I had.

I chatted with and profiled Devin a few years back for Canadian Running magazine and thought he was an amazing trail runner and he had some amazing trail run photos! I became a dad about the same time as he did...be I think he has adjusted much better than I. This is Devin.

Devin Featherstone

A runner profiled back in 2015, life has changed for the Calgary fireman and trail runner. He is now a dad.

Devin grew up playing hockey and only started really running when he joined the Calgary fire department. He began running and got into trail running and lots of it. Devin went from 5ks to 100milers.

Devin: *"I love the drive, mental focus and the suffer fest of running very technical trails. I have race races all over Alberta, British Columbia, Oregon, Hawaii and Hong Kong. It is a way for me to see the landscapes in a different way. Hawaii was HURT 100 miler and my wife was 35 weeks pregnant crewing me, she then had out beautiful boy Kai 2 weeks later when we arrived home. It has changed our lives for the better and couldn't imagine a day without him. He has pushed us to explore and show him a crazy life all in his first year. Kai was at the finish line in Hong Kong in October to give me a smile and a big kiss."*

Races Devin has run

Squamish 50 -50

HURT 100 Miler – Top 10 finish

Lost Souls 100km – Two time winner

Gorge Falls 100km

Lantau 70km

Iron Legs 50 miler

Carlgary Marathon – 4th overall, 9th overall

MEC Half marathon with a stroller 1:22 hr\min 2nd place overall

What was the hardest part for you – transitioning to running dad life?

"The biggest thing was the upper body that you think you have but when you push a stroller around you really realize that all those tiny muscles that you usually don't use are being used nonstop. Even your hands holding onto the bar to steer takes its toll and you need to switch. I was a learning curve for sure but one that you need to take baby steps. I think my first run with the stroller was when my son was napping, it ended up being about 24km because I had to keep moving for him to sleep. That was by far the hardest part was once I started I had to go until he woke up but as we did it more often it became easier to know when you could stop or routes you could pick to make it fun for you and him."

What have you enjoyed the most about being a dad?

"The thing I love about being a dad is all the time off from my job as a fire fighter. It allows me to spend so much time with Kai and really see every little thing he goes through. The funny phases like loving sunglasses or birds. It truly melts my heart to think of a day without him. Kai didn't slow me down he has kept me going. Keeping me running and exploring in the mountains. It is an opportunity where I get to do it with him and show him the kind of life his father loves. To me that is the best part of being a dad and capturing those moments through photos."

How has your running and life changed after becoming a running dad?

"Life has changed, as it would with anyone. You now have a human that depends on you. It can be scary to most. I use to be able to get up and go to the mountains to run all the time or run whenever I want. It has changed to the point where you have to plan a lot better. You have to be able to do what is best for them. I have planned runs where I have had to cancel them and run on the treadmill later. Trail running is my true love but having Kai has made me appreciate having a treadmill. I will run on a treadmill so he can have a better nap or stay warmer inside. I still get to the mountains once a week but to me its okay and wouldn't trade it for anything."

What advice would you give another dad to be (who runs) about what to expect when the little one arrives?

"I would give the advice to not listen to the people who will tell you YOU WONT BE ABLE TO DO THAT! I had that a lot and it was my goal to prove them wrong and I think I have done a damn good job of it. If you are passionate about running you will do it. Run with a stroller ease into it, dress the kids accordingly and pack food and things to make life easier. Know you might have to cut your run short if a meltdown happens. If you want to keep running you might need to run a 5am before work or the kid is up, you might need to sacrifice and run on a treadmill which is called the dreadmill to me. My biggest advice is don't make excuses to not do it, because you can do anything. I prove it daily from

running, hiking, biking, ski touring, cross country skiing, snow shoeing with Kai and you can too."

Devin you inspire this running dad. Run on my friend.

You can catch Devin on Instagram @dfeatherstone or on his blog, Tiny Big Adventure.

This was published on my blog in June 2017. Devin continues to run and can be seen being an extremely active runningdad on social media.

There are many reasons people run. Sometimes a personal cause or situation causes people to look for a way to take a journey raise awareness or learn about themselves. Sometimes they do epic runs, other times it's just a personal challenge.

I have respect for those who do good while running no matter the cause. There is something about someone putting something on the line and sweating to try to help others.

"When you are balanced and when you listen and attend to the needs of your body, mind, and spirit, your natural beauty comes out." - Christy Turlington

Model Christy Turlington Burns on running the 2016 Boston marathon

Christy Turlington Burns is a mother, social entrepreneur, model and founder of the maternal health organization, Every Mother Counts. She is also a runner.

In 2011, the face that has graced so many magazines lined up for the New York City marathon to race. Turlington Burns is now set to run the 2016 Boston Marathon. She qualified with a time of 3:46 at the London Marathon.

Turlington Burns has been recognized as one of Time's 100 Most Influential People and Glamour's Woman of the Year. Aside from running, founding Every Mother Counts and her modeling career, she's also a member of the Harvard Medical School Global Health Council and on the advisory Board of New York University's Nursing School. She holds a BA from NYU and has studied public health at Columbia University.

She is also running the Boston marathon for the cause she founded.

Every Mother Counts

Having endured a childbirth complication herself, Christy was compelled to direct the documentary, No Woman, No Cry about maternal health challenges that impact the lives of millions of women around the world.

Every Mother Counts supports programs that improve access to comprehensive maternity care in Haiti, Uganda, Bangladesh, India, Tanzania, Guatemala and the United States. Since 2012, Every Mother Counts has impacted over 400,000 lives by linking women to proper care during and after pregnancy and childbirth.

We had the chance to ask her about her running and her work.

Why did you decide to run the Boston marathon?

In my mind, Boston always felt out of my league. Every Mother Counts had a small team presence there in 2013 and I followed our runners right up to the moment the race was stopped after the bombing and chaos that ensued. Some of those runners returned the following year, so we have had a couple of runners representing EMC the last few years.

Last winter, I started training for the London marathon and just before heading over, the thought of qualifying for Boston did cross my mind. As soon as I finished and shared my time (3:46 – PR for me), I heard from people that I had qualified for Boston and that's when I decided I would run it this year.

You ran your first marathon in New York in 2011. What has your running been like since then?

I have run a marathon each year since that first one in NYC in 2011. I have now done NYC, Chicago and London. I also trained for NYC in 2012 when it was cancelled due to Hurricane Sandy. I did not seriously consider myself a runner until after my second marathon, but I do now. I run all year round and sign up for half-marathons in between the full marathons to keep me motivated. Last year, we participated in the Kilimanjaro Half and Full Marathon in Tanzania and I just returned from Haiti where we ran a 20K in Jacmel. Every Mother Counts supports programs that improve access to essential maternity care in both of those countries.

How do you fit training into a busy schedule?

It certainly helps that Every Mother Counts is also my job so I can incorporate training into my workday. I travel a lot so planning my long runs around that and other commitments

can be a challenge, but I incorporate training into my
schedule just as I would a meeting.

What is the attraction do running? What do you enjoy about it?

*I ran as a child in other sports and periodically as an adult
for exercise, which I didn't enjoy as much. I have rediscovered
the joy in running and the solitude and peace of mind it gives
me. Running is a spiritual practice for me that integrates
mind, body and soul.*

What is the link between running and Every Mother Counts?

*In 2011, a year after Every Mother Counts launched, we were
offered a handful of spots in the NYC Marathon. I knew in
that moment this was a challenge I wanted to take on. As I
was training, I realized that running has a lot of similarities
to the experience of pregnancy and labor both physically and
mentally. It has also been a powerful way to educate the
public about one of the biggest barriers girls and women face
when bringing life into the world: distance. Many women
live miles away from healthcare providers and facilities, with
extremely limited access to transportation. Poor road
conditions and nonexistent or unreliable public
transportation make travel difficult and unsafe. Emergency
care may be 40 kilometres or more away and ambulances are
rare. Women often have to make that trek by foot, while in
labor. All of the funds raised from our runners are invested
into programs that help break down these barriers and bring*

women closer to the basic maternal healthcare they need to survive.

A four-time marathon finisher, Christy resides in New York City where she lives with her husband, filmmaker Edward Burns, and their two children.

This article was originally published in Canadian Running magazine in April 2016.

Running is a simple sport I that it is not overly complicated. Explaining the reason you run or how it makes you feel however can be difficult. There are a few amongst the crowd who enjoy lacing up and can put a pen to paper or type at the keyboard and explain it to others.

These are the running writers.

"It's very hard at the beginning to understand that the whole idea is not to beat the other runners. Eventually, you learn that the competition is against the little voice inside you that wants you to quit." —George Sheehan

Talking Running

Meeting another running writer

"Movies are great but nothing will replace the written word – that allows your mind to add colour and character to the story."

Recently while at a local running shop (Sports4 – College Square location) – I came across a book written by a local runner – about running. I was automatically interested to check it out and find out more about the author. Like some sort of weird bloodhound on the scent of another running writer!

The book

Unspoken, Or the Unrefined Art of Communicating at the Top of Your Lungs and Through the Bottom of Your Feet

By Larry McCloskey

176 Pages • ISBN: 978-0995336008 – by Dog-Eared Books

Available on Amazon in Kindle or paperback

The novel is written by fellow running dad and Ottawa native Larry McCloskey. The book was printed by the independent publisher, Dog-Eared Books, which McCloskey co-founded.

The book is about a dad, his daughter, running, romance and life (which is always changing and challenging us). I am not a fan of the long version of the title but like 'Unspoken'. The two main characters are a talented local single running dad who excels at racing but not so much in communicating, and his daughter who loves her dad but is dealing with a complex world around her. I sense that there is a lot of Larry and his experiences in this book. I won't give away too much of the story for that is for you (the reader of this review) to go find out.

The writer and runner

So I sniffed out the author of the book (Larry) and we coordinated a meeting to talk about him, his running and his writing. I liked the idea of meeting someone else who shared the same passions – and he was also a running dad too!

Talking Running

We met in Larry's corner office (with a great view) at Carleton university and I automatically knew I had met another real runner and writer – who's passion for both equaled my own – different but very similar. Oh and he was wearing a shirt! Larry swears he does occasionally wear a shirt while running but said (while laughing) that the ones he found – well he is shirtless. The photos of him in his youth and in his 60s both show a very fit individual).

Writer: Coming from an Irish family, with an English Lit degree – Larry works as Director of the Paul Menton Centre for Students with Disabilities. His writing like my own is something he does on the side. He has written a few other books (all for children/youth) including, The Dog Who Cried Snake and Tom Thomson's Last Paddle – but this is his first where running is the main topic.

Runner: Lacing up for the first time to get fit and stop smoking Larry found a love and not just something to do. Larry was more than a 'jogger' as well. Running turned to racing and in the 1980s, training hard but not the 100-mile weeks that were popular at the time (for almost everyone) – Larry got fast! At the famous Around The Bay race (30K) (oldest race in North America) he was 2nd in 1986 (1:40.17) and in 1988 was 3rd (1:40.13). he however was not a youngster and started running a bit later than most – in his 40s he was still running hard and fast. In his 40s Larry blistered a 1:07 half-marathon at the World Masters World marathon championships (a time/performance he was actually disappointed with).

Half marathon: 1:07

10K: 30:20

We chatted about writing, running, being dads and liking to help people. I liked Larry – we grabbed a sandwich and then parted ways. I had a book to read.

Book review (my thoughts)

Larry and I share many things in common (running, writing, dads, like helping) and I can almost see myself writing a book similar to this. I liked it because of who I am and because I can relate. I think a young reader who has a dad who runs will really relate to this – and kids who grow up in single parent families and deal with the complexities of life in general – will get this book. It is about running but not at the same time.

This is a book written with heart and experience and worth a read. Run and write on Larry!

Talking Running

"Life like running is something that must be done one step at a time, it has ups and downs, curves and often unexpected challenges – each of us have a different journey/race to run."

Larry still runs, but now more to stay in shape and lives in Ottawa with his wife and three daughters.

First published on my personal blog in February 2018.

There is something about running, whether the endorphins or the sweat taking away negative thought, but few runners look mad or in a foul mood after a run. Running seems to produce happy people. Its good for the body, mind and soul.

Happy, positive people also seem to want to help others. I know so many runners who use their love for the sport and combine with a need to lend a hand to others.

"You have to wonder at times what you're doing out there. Over the years, I've given myself a thousand reasons to keep running, but it always comes back to where it started. It comes down to self-satisfaction and a sense of achievement."
— Steve Prefontaine,

Always doing good on foot – Nick *Brindisi*

"Running always seems to bring out the good in people and often people do good by running." – Noel Paine

As far back as I can remember I knew running was connected to not just seeing who was the fastest but also doing good. I was a young kid when Terry Fox ran across Canada with one prosthetic leg to raise money to help fight cancer. Now there are charity runs for lots of causes and people challenging themselves for personal causes (I have done this). If more people are doing them – does it take away from these runs? I don't think so.

This is a profile of a running friend and fellow runningdad. This is my friend Nick – who runs for himself but also does a lot of good on foot and in the running community.

Photos above: Nick and I during our 258km 2.5day Rideau Trail run.

Nick Brindisi

Nick is a 55-year-old father of 2 boys aged 25 and 21 and husband to Susan (all whom I have met) and lives in Collingwood, Ontario (Canada). Nick is my height and weight and another endurance runner – also liking to partake in the occasional very long trail ultra.

We are both very similar as well as started running middle distance on the track and then did our best marathons (to date) in our 30s. I started running in grade seven and Nick in middle school.

Nick is the President of the Georgian Triangle Running Club, race director for a Collingwood half-marathon held in the fall and coach teens with depression under the Team Unbreakable program of Cameron Helps.

Nick and I met through a mutual friend when I was looking for someone foolish enough to join me for a very long 40th birthday run in 2015. We ran for 2.5 days together over 258-kilometres of road, trail, path and bike path (the Rideau Trail) after only a few minutes of introduction. We became friends over those few days.

Nick's running

10 KM – 41:30

Half Marathon – 1:25

Marathon – 3:15

50K with 10,000 feet vertical climb --- 5:03

75 KM hilly charity road run for hospital -8:16

80 km with 12,000 feet vertical climb- 10:44

100 KM hilly road charity run for hospital- 10:48

100 miles (Sinister 7) 27:29

"I run because it's who I am not just a sport. I have found my place in the universe and it is a metaphor for other endeavours in life that keeps me on pace, on target, and the happiness it generates is a beautiful thing. It's calming, it's

Talking Running

physical benefits are many and it helps me be an ambassador for so many programs and people." – Nick

Nick is an ambassador for 2XU – a brand of compression and sportswear.

Running Good

Ok so hold onto your running tights friends – in addition to all the running and stuff above – Nick does more.

Nick is also a partner in Aspire Sports Kenya which helps athletes pursue their dreams, and coaches 5 athletes in Kapsabet Kenya – all 2:11 to 2:15 marathoners. This running man also imports handmade products from Nepal to aid in earthquake relief. To mark his 55th birthday my friend Nick ran 55-kilometres on a cold November day to raise money to help a local women's shelter. This is one cool guy.

Nick's plan and projects include a run to Everest base camp in the Himalayas, solo Kilimanjaro, create an ultra trail race around Mount Kenya, return to Sinister 7 (Ultra) to better his time, UTMB, return to Kenya to coach orphans and street kids.

I am hoping to try and catch up with Nick for at least one adventure – I can't keep up!

You can find Nick on his website or on Twitter @NickBrindisi

Nick continues to run and race. In 2018 he ran the Haliburton 100-miler and a number of other races and ultras, fundraisers, directed his Collingwood race and managed time for the 2018 Ottawa marathon which I paced him through.

Age is something that follows all of us through life and tends to slow us down over time. How we adjust and handle the changes of life often dictates how we run and race. I have seen many an older runner who looks years younger than his age and who has double the determination and guts of someone half his age.

"Age is no barrier. It's a limitation you put on your mind." —
Jackie Joyner-Kersee

Grandpa kicking your butt

"One's never too old to start again." – Ed Whitlock

Grandpas are supposed to be slow moving, friendly characters who give out candy and wear warm sweaters. Our grandfathers are not supposed to be capable of lacing up their running shoes and kicking our butt at the local road race.

People are always saying that age is simply a number, but it is often are bodies that seem to argue it is more than that. Strength, speed and flexibility among other things are things that seem harder to maintain, as one gets older. Then there exceptions. Here is the story of one American grandpa who can kick the butt of those his own age and quite a few in the younger age categories at every race he enters. Meet Gene.

Gene Dykes

Gene is 5'10", 140lbs and 70-years old. He is a retired computer programmer, is married, two daughters and is a grandfather in Philadelphia. Aside from running, Gene says he likes gardening, cooking and the occasional golf game. Sounds like your typical retiree past times, but Gene's running makes up for his quiet hobbies. At 70, no one suspects that the white-haired runner with glasses is capable of unleashing a 19-min 5k and is capable of running 200-miles!

The running bug bit back when Gene as a little bit younger and was growing up in Canton, Ohio - but most likely weighed the same at age 14. He ran track in high school and college but only "jogged" recreationally as an adult.

"My current career in running began in 2004 when I started running with some friends after a 6-year injury layoff, and I ran my first race in 2006. My first marathon was the 2006 NYC (and I've done 106 more since then, including ultramarathons)."

When he got back into more training and racing, he really got into it. Aside from the shorter races and marathons he started to run he also liked going beyond the marathon. In 2017 he ran the Tahoe 200, Bigfoot 200, and Moab 240, that is two 200-mile races and one 240-mile race! Gene describes himself as goal oriented and is clearly super-determined when he sets his mind to something.

"I pursue goals with enthusiasm, but I'm not afraid to change horses midstream. I was enthusiastic about chemistry, but when I discovered computer programming, I completely changed my career path. I loved golf, but when my first child was born, I gave up golf cold turkey. It's hard to imagine anything that would consume me more than running, but I certainly wouldn't be surprised if there is something else I'll be pursuing whole-heartedly in the near future."

Personal Bests

* All of them except the 5K were set at age 69 or 70.

200 miles	98:10:22
100 miles	23:41:22
100K	16:16:43
50 miles	9:47:32
50K	4:52:51
Marathon	2:55:18
Half	1:26:34
10 miles	1:03:01
15K	1:00:27
10K	39:02

5 miles	32:31
8K	30:48
5K	19:01
3K	11:22
1500m	5:17

In October 2018, at age 70, Gene missed breaking Canadian Ed Whitlock's 70-74 age group record of 2:54:48 at the Scotiabank Toronto Waterfront Marathon by 34 seconds. He is the only other person in the world besides Whitlock to run a sub-3 marathon at the age of 70. It was the second sub-3 hour marathon. Just after turning 70 in the spring at the Rotterdam Marathon, he ran 2:57.

I was amazed to hear someone else had come close to Ed's marathon record and was intrigued to know more. I contacted Gene and he was eager to talk running.

What drives you to keep racing and pushing yourself at an age where many people hang up their running shoes?

"When I decide to do something, it's often the case that much of the satisfaction is derived from giving it my best effort. I'm not content to just participate. In the past, I have had the same kind of enthusiasm for golf and bowling that I now have for running. The competition in running is especially geared to measure success against those of similar age, so the thrill of competition does not decrease, as one gets older."

What is the biggest change you have noticed with your running, as you have gotten older?

"I've been running competitively for 12 years now, and each year I've gotten faster!"

"Each year I compete against myself from the previous year. I try to outdo whatever I've done the previous year by running further or more often. Pretty soon I'm going to run out of toppers! It's hard to outdo the Triple Crown of 200's for example, but I'll give it a go in 2019 by running a 100-mile race and a 200-mile race in the same month."

What is your secret to racing well at over 70?

"Not having raced a lot earlier in life. All the big names in running from long ago who are now my age are nowhere to be seen."

"Working with an incredible coach who knows way better than I do what I'm capable of."

Who inspires you?

"Really, nothing inspires me more than trying to beat that guy in the Mirror's (newspaper) results from last year."

What are your goals or running dreams for the future?

"I'd love to win the M120 age group at Boston. Let's see... since I've won my age group the last 3 years, that would mean I might win 53 years in a row!

There are so many awesome ultras, stage races, and adventure runs all over the world – I want to run as many as I can."

Most runners may never be as fast as Gene but maybe emulating his drive and passion may bring success and personal bests. Running always seems to have another challenge at every turn. Never stop challenging yourself.

Shortly after finishing this piece on Gene for this book, he entered and ran the Jacksonville Marathon in Florida on December 15, 2018. He ran an amazing 2:54:23 that was 25 seconds under Canadian Ed Whitlock's World Record for men over 70. Shortly after the race he found out the record was not valid as the Jacksonville Marathon is not USATF-sanctioned. Still damn fast and he still ran the fastest ever marathon by someone over 70, it is just not an official record.

Where you come from seems to have little to do with how fast you run. You can be an African, a Canadian or a Scandinavian and still be a good runner. Whether altitude or running in waist deep snow to make you tough – running seems more about the training, the mental toughness and just getting out there.

Its about who you are and what you do not where you are.

"Run often. Run long. But never outrun your joy of running."
—Julie Isphording

Talking Running

Running on the Rock

"Everyone runner has a story to tell."

I have chattered back and forth with a elite runner from Newfoundland long enough (did meet in person once) – so decided it was time to profile him and introduce him to others.

David Freake

Newfoundland is sometimes referred to as the rock – perhaps referring to its hard, rocky terrain and this is where David Freake runs. Calling, St. John's home he works full time as a technical sales representative and account manager for a

BioPharma company. When not at work he can very often be found lacing up his running shoes and flying down the road or around a local track, and on weekends he often is winning road races. Freake is an elite-level road racer who unlikely many others drawn to the big cities of Montreal, Toronto or Vancouver to train has stayed on 'the rock' to run.

A Brooks sponsored athlete, the lean runner with a great smile only picked up the sport in the summer of 2010 as a way to get into shape after what he describes as a fairly sedentary university student lifestyle. Spending the first couple of years just running, gaining experience and chasing other runners around he says he started to then look into how to train, to get faster.

"I became fascinated by the physiology of running and how when we stress our bodies we see adaptation. I made some decent progress in 2012 but it was really 2013 that I began training the way an athlete should. I have a fantastic coach in

Jeremiah Johnston who I began working with in 2015. Under his tutelage I feel like I will be able to make consistent progress and become a much more developed runner. I have lofty goals in this sport, but I know that I can't rush things. So I will build upon the foundation I have and make small steps towards my long term goals in a seasonal/yearly fashion."

And David has gotten faster as his personal bests below can testify to.

Personal Bests

14:56 for 5km

24:07 for 8km

31:07 for 10km

68:47 for the half marathon

Despite being miles away from the big city hubs and where there are often large competitive track or road racing clubs – Freake has found a way with the help of his coach to run and push himself. And it is not only the distance from big city races or clubs that can make running on the rock a challenge. He describes running in Newfoundland as 50/50. He says from April to November it's fantastic with amazing trails, a 200m indoor facility and an 8 lane Canada Games 400m outdoor track (in St. John's) but winter is what's difficult. Echoing what most Canadians see on the weather channel, Newfoundland gets very cold temperatures, plenty of snow and high winds. Freake says he gets friendly with the treadmill for much of the frigid winters when outdoor running just does not make sense or is unsafe.

David is sponsored by Brooks Canada also supported by Smith Optics, CEP Compression and LeanFit.

What is your favourite Newfoundland race?

"My favorite race on the rock would have to be "The Tely 10 Mile". It's our cities version of the Boston Marathon, everyone comes out to show support and lot's of fast runner's like Matt Loiselle come down to race it. Over the past 5 years it has grown from 2500 finishers to well over 5000 last year. After the race or a training run I like to grab some sushi with friends and training partners at Sun Sushi in downtown St. John's which has a great view of the harbor."

What drives you to keep running faster?

"I think what drives me to run faster and train harder is an inherit drive to push past goals and see just how much I can get out of my body. I was never a runner growing up so to have started in my early 20's rather than my teen years it's fun to compete against those with a more decorated and substantial running pedigree and see where I stack up."

What are your goals for 2017 and beyond?

"My goals for 2017 are to run 30:30 for 10km on the roads as well as break our provincial half and full marathon records which are a modest 67:22 and 2:24:17. (our records for the 10k and under are untouchable as they are held by Olympian

Paul McCloy. (For reference he's run 13:27 for 5000m and 27:XX on the road and track for 10k, still holding the Canadian 10k road record to this day."

Although Freake does run and race at home he can be found hitting the mainland now and again to run his favourite competitive races like the Vancouver Sun Run, Goodlife Toronto Half and Ottawa race weekend, 5km national championships and the Toronto marathon and Canadian Cross-country nationals in the fall. Keep an eye out for this fast Newfoundland runner.

This piece was published on my personal blog in July 2017. David continues to train and race. In 2017 he was the 8th Canadian at the Toronto waterfront Marathon and 3rd at the Montreal Rock and Roll half-marathon. In 2018 he an indoor personal best for 3000m (8:33), won a number of local road races on the Rock and was the 2018 winner of the Toronto Goodlife marathon in 2:33:57. David says he is in PB shape and has his eyes on a personal best and a provincial record early in 2019 and will be toeing the line of the Houston marathon on January 20th, 2019.

Find David on his blog, on Twitter @Davefreake or Instagram @Davefreake. David is sponsored by Brooks, Smith Optics, CEP, LeanFit and Suunto.

Running and racing can make you feel fit, happy and like you are achieving things. This is the physical. Sometimes you must also take care of the mental you. Going out for a run can take away some stress and help you think but it may not solve your problems.

Sometimes talking about what you do not want to talk about is what you need to do. It's about balance. Physical and mental health.

"Our running shoes have magic in them. The power to transform a bad day into a good day; frustration into speed; self-doubt into confidence; chocolate cake into muscle." — Mina Samuels

Run Therapy?

"Running has always been therapy for me – it just took me years to realize it." – Noel Paine

In my travels on social media I am always bumping into other runners and finding great stories to share – often too many for me to tackle. Here is one about a Canadian runner, psychologist and someone who has combined normal talk therapy with lacing up the shoes for a run or walk.

Using running as part of therapy

Meet Kristy McConnell. She is the founder of Off the Beaten Path Psychology and Wellness. She is a Registered Psychologist with the College of Alberta Psychologists and helps those dealing with mental health issues in Calgary and Airdrie, Alberta (Canada).She is also a runner and mom.

Off the Beaten Path introduces unique mental health treatment methods that utilizes movement by walking or running together during the therapy session. I have always found there is a link between body and mind and running has helped this runningdad dig himself out of depression – so I was interested to talk to Kristy.

I asked Kristy about herself and her unique way of helping people.

"I started my career as a special education teacher a long time ago. I loved working with the tough kids, but sometimes I didn't feel prepared to work with the grief that many of my parents experienced on a regular basis. I went on to earn my Masters of Counseling Psychology. Currently I am a psychologist who is interested in using movement through running and walking as a catalyst for the work that we do within the therapeutic relationship."

I then asked Kristy about her running.

"I remember going for runs with my Dad as early as grade 3. Eventually, he would ride his bike beside me and challenge me to sprint to the next light post. I never really liked that. I'm definitely built for long runs, not sprinting. I joke on my website that the only top finish I have in the record books is once in grade 7 on the beep test. It's true. I'll never forget that. Kicked the soccer player's arses. There have been times that

I've stepped away from running, but I've always come back to it. In high-school I used to run the same 5km loop after school a few times a week to cope with... well... being in high-school."

After having my third child, I started doing half marathons. Running was something that felt like it was just for me, while at the same time carrying the added benefit of helping me be a better wife, mother, friend, and psychologist. Soon enough, I was itching to do a full marathon, but knew that I'd need training. About 5 years ago, I was at a week-long professional development conference on trauma and addiction. Every morning they had facilitated runs with a running coach.

That's where I met Charles Miron of Solo Sports Systems. That August, with his help, I completed my first full marathon: the Edmonton Marathon. I've since completed 2 more and intend to do my 4th this May at the Blue Nose

Talking Running

Marathon in Nova Scotia (my great-great-great uncle was George Rhuland who built the first Bluenose). Personal best marathon- Vancouver 2016- 4:15. PB half marathon- Okanagan half marathon 1:53. Charles is still my coach and won the Fire and Ice 250km Ultra Marathon in Iceland last year, so in my mind, he's kind of a big deal.

Then I asked Kristy about her unique approach to helping those with mental health by incorporating running and walking into your therapy.

"So often we hear about the positive benefits of exercise on our mental health. In fact, doctors have started to prescribe physical activity on their scripts. If you've been anxious or depressed, you know that sometimes writing it down on a piece of paper isn't enough. I've often joked with my running coach that I wish my employee benefits would allow me to claim his support, because after all, I feel good during and after running. That's sort of the genesis of where Off the Beaten Path came from. I then started to research whether or not anyone else out there was doing it. Sure enough, I found a few: Run Walk Talk in California and Dynamic Running Therapy Britain. I connected with Sepideh of Run Walk Talk, and continue to consult with her today. Although California's climate is much more conducive to running therapy, I knew that Calgarians would be up for it despite our climate.

Seeking help for anxiety, depression, relationship issues, can be hugely intimidating. Sometimes, sitting across from someone in a stuffy office is just too much. Walking or running alongside someone is far less abrasive. There is less

Talking Running

pressure. In running, we can be mindful. Mindful of the mind-body connection and how the two works together. Then we can also be curious about how the mind and body work together in other settings: with our partners, kids, and colleagues. If the client comes out running at a full Greyhound speed, what does that say about their tendencies in life? Do they give too much of themselves too quickly? Are they quick to dismiss the cues their body is signaling because they don't want to disappoint? Running therapy is about getting off of the proverbial coach and using running as a catalyst and metaphor within the work that needs to be done in the client's life.

I think if I was in the Calgary area I would head out for a run with Kristy. I like her approach and it certainly strikes home – to what I have learned about myself and how running has helped me.

When not running and being a psychologist, Kristy loves being with her family, being active (mountain biking, snowboarding, and cross-country skiing), has recently discovered of paddle boarding and has a love for music.

Off the Beaten Path website: www.obpwellness.com

Kristy on Twitter: @obpwellness

Remember you are never alone running friends and never give in. Run happy.

This was published on my personal blog in January 2018.

Life can seem like a marathon. Sometimes you arrive at a certain point in your life or face a challenge that seems insurmountable. The goal or where you want to be seems so far away.

Like a marathon you start slow, you have a plan and keep going even when the benefits from all the work you put in seem small. Things add up and you see progress.

Before you know it you have arrived at the finish line. Sometimes it just takes time and effort.

"Running taught me valuable lessons. In cross-country competition, training counted more than intrinsic ability, and I could compensate for a lack of natural aptitude with diligence and discipline. I applied this in everything I did." - Nelson Mandela

Losing 170lbs and gaining a passion

"Sometimes people say I inspire them because of a quote, a picture I post or after reading about one of my runs – but it is the runners I meet and profile who inspire me."

Melinda Howard is someone I noticed and connected with on Twitter – I found out her story and asked her if she wanted to share. I hope you find her as inspiring and interesting as I did.

Meet Melinda

Melinda was born in 1962 as the oldest of 2 children in Des Moines, Iowa. She went to high school, then college and got married and had 2 children – and did not run.

She says the running thing started in 2011. She wanted to lose a bit of weight and when her sister asked her to join a "couch to 5k" running program, she simply saw it as a way to lose weight faster —she never knew it would change her life.

She completed the 5k and was soon invited by friends to run a 12k race (a distance she would never have imagined possible not that long before). She finished the 12k and made running friends she says she still has to this day.

The running continued and soon Melinda was finding that 5ks and 10ks were fun but she wanted to see how far she could go. In 2012, a year after starting running she ran a half-marathon. Her first marathon came not long after and she ran the Mt. Desert Island marathon with friends and found herself head over heels in love with running.

From runner to ultramarathoner

Believe it or not, before she had even finished her first marathon she had already registered for a 50-mile race. She was hooked and had a desire to see how far she could go. Back from the marathon she was soon out training for her first ultra.

Perhaps with too much running too soon and as a new runner she had pushed too hard and soon found herself injured. She ended up limping around on crutches for the winter of 2013. But she was as determined as ever.

She got back to running, got a coach and since her injury in 2013 has 12 marathons and 4 Ultra Marathons plus lots of HM's and shorter distance races. She says she loves to run.

Melinda's Running

Holds the 10 Mile Mississippi State Record for 53 year old women

2nd AG 50-55 Tanglefoot Half Marathon 2014

2nd AG 50-55 Pilgrimage Half Marathon 2015

1st AG 50-55 Tanglefoot Half Marathon 2015

2nd AG 50-59 Green Street Mile 2015

50M PR: Brazos Bend 50M (12:46:56) 7th

50K PR: MS50 Trail Run (7:04:15) 9th overall Female

Marathon PR: Mississippi River Marathon. (5:05:15)

Half Marathon PR: Viking Half Marathon. (2:15:00)

What was the hardest hurdle going from non-runner and overweight to runner and how did you overcome it?

"Well, when I first started running, MFH (My Favorite Husband) ran with me every single training run and every single race. On Saturday mornings, we would go to our local running club. Our club has some elite level runners (for real elites!) and I was incredibly intimidated by them. Truth be told, I'm still intimidated by them!!! They seem to glide over the road. It's a beautiful thing to see. That being said, I'm very well aware of my limitations and some of them I feel like I'm being judged. I've seen this group welcome many, MANY runners of different shapes and sizes so I know it's just me."

"You asked how I overcame it? Instead of comparing myself to them (some of them I was old enough to be their mom), I discovered my own strengths and focused on those. I found out that I stink at 5K's but do pretty well at Ultra's. I began to build a solid mileage base so I could do the long stuff."

"At the beginning, as an overweight runner, I worked hard to eat smart, run smart and continue to trim up and drop weight. After 3.5 years of this, I wasn't an overweight runner

anymore! I still, sometimes, have a hard time not seeing myself as an overweight runner. Isn't that crazy? We're so hard on ourselves."

How does running make you feel and have you learned anything about yourself from it?

"Running makes me feel free. It helps me be confident. I never knew I could be confident. I had often been made to feel inferior so this was something alien to me. Over time I've learned that there's a lot more grit and determination in me to succeed than I never knew I had."

How do ultras differ from "normal" races and why do you run beyond 26.2 miles?

How do ultras differ. This made me giggle. Ultras are a totally different creature. They're much more laid back. They're still competitive but you don't live and die by your time on the clock. You want to finish. You'd like to finish well but you really want to finish.

Most ultra runners I've met don't ask you your finishing time. They will ask, "Did you finish?" That's what counts! Did you have what it took to grind out the miles? There's respect if you can do that! If somebody asks you your finishing time, I'd be willing to bet that they're new to Ultras and are there to see what Ultra running is all about. I'd also bet you they're a marathoner. LOL!!!

Why do I run beyond 26.2~,because nine times out of ten, I'm one of the oldest women on the course. There's not many women my age out there running 50M or trying 100M. It makes me feel badass. Is it wrong to admit that? LOL!!! I have a great deal of respect and admiration for women my age and older who are out there on the trails pounding out the miles. It's not easy but it's totally awesome!!!

Any advice to someone considering lacing up?

"Advice? Lace up those shoes and get moving!!! If I can drop 170lbs by eating smart and moving more, anybody can do it! I was on oxygen 24/7 and couldn't tie my own shoes. I had to have one of my children or my husband do that kind of stuff for me. Walking across a room was a major ordeal. You just have to set your mind to it. Grind your teeth and get started...and stick with it! As much as I dislike this phrase, it's true: Patience is a virtue.

Someday you'll realize that you can see your feet again! Someday it'll dawn on you that you just bet over and tied your own shoes! Do you know what you'll do next? You'll do the Happy Dance because you're making progress! Celebrate the little victories because they eventually add up to big victories!!!"

"I wish those starting the best of luck."

Find Melinda on Twitter: @MelindaHoward4

This was published on my personal blog in April 2017. Melinda continues to run with her dog and often with a tire dragging behind her.

There is something about running to support someone else or when you run for a reason that seems to lighten the load. It makes the running more important and yet at the same time gives you more strength to run.

Talking Running

"God has given me the ability. The rest is up to me. Believe. Believe. Believe." – Billy Mills

Running as a Battery

"You realize how powerful the mind is, and I sort of have this belief that if you believe something and you will your body to do it, you CAN do it. It might just hurt a lot." – Blaine Penny

If you were passed in a marathon by someone dressed as a battery it might have made you laugh or cry and had you known the story or man behind you, inspired you.

At the 2018 Toronto Waterfront marathon there were many runners in tights or running shorts but only one dressed like an AA battery. With his head jutting out and looking like it would have been difficult to walk in, this runner was running rather than wobbling along at pedestrian pace. Dressed as a copper and green battery this runner ran a world record for the fastest man ever to run a marathon dressed as a battery, and by more than an hour with an amazing time of 2:59:58.

Talking Running

Blaine Penny

Blaine is the Co-Founder and CEO of MitoCanada, is a competitive marathoner (2:29 PB) and ultra marathoner, cross-country skier, cyclist, 3-time Canadian Ultramarathon Champion, 5-time Guinness World Record holder, and 2015 North American winner of the Wings for Life World Run. He's also an ambassador with Team Salomon – Suunto Running. He is driven and has a reason for his running.

Blaine grew up in the small town of Gambo, Newfoundland and was adopted at a young age along with his eldest brother. Blaine has four sisters in his adoptive family and later found out he had five more in his biological family (whom he met later in life). He was involved in nearly every sport, from track and field to volleyball to badminton, and like most Canadian kids wanted to play in the NHL. His first real competitive sport and passion was cross-country skiing. He skied well enough to make the Newfoundland provincial team and represented his province competing in many national events including the Canada Games in 1991 and 1995.

Ten years ago, Blaine's son (Evan) tragically suffered an unexplained brain injury overnight and went from being a perfectly typical 4-year-old boy to a spastic quadriplegic (who could no longer walk, talk or eat) as a result of mitochondrial disease. Over the past ten years, Blaine has poured thousands of volunteer hours into helping raise awareness and funds for mitochondrial disease. Blaine has been formally recognized with several awards including the Dave Kelly Live Award, Calgary Top 40 Under 40, recognized as a Kickass Canadian, and attended the prestigious Governor General's Canadian Leadership Conference.

Running

Switching from skiing to running happened because of his son. With parenthood comes less time and Blaine found he was able to squeeze running into a busy schedule easier than skiing. Blaine was also successful at running and by 2007 was not only running but competing in races longer than marathons (ultras). He won races, set course records and in 2010 (as well as 2011 and 2012) won the Iron Legs 50-miler, which doubled as the Canadian 50-Mile Ultramarathon Championship.

Blaine's drive to start MitoCanada and often his motivation to run for this cause is because his son Evan suffers from mitochondrial disease. Shortly after he started running ultras was when he realized the connection between the disease his son had and running. Evan's life as a result of this energy sapping disease is an ultramarathon and sadly involves a lot of pain and suffering. Blaine found solace, strength and inspiration by running long distances to be the best father he could be in order to provide Evan with the best care and quality of life possible. The suffering, focus and determination required to run at an elite level provides the mental strength and determination Blaine needs to get through the challenges of caring for Evan, while having hope and continuing to move forward despite the pain and obstacles in his way.

Blaine's reason to run

Blaine's son Evan woke up one morning with stomach pain. Blaine and his wife took him to the Alberta Children's Hospital. The doctors at first thought Evan was suffering from appendicitis, so they scheduled emergency surgery. Just as Evan was being wheeled into the operation, Blaine recalls his son looking him in the eye and asking: "Daddy, can we play together again sometime?" Those are the last words Evan has spoken since 2008.

Evan did not wake up from the surgery. Something was seriously wrong. It was soon found out that he had suffered brain damage. Evan was eventually diagnosed with mitochondrial disease. The doctors never determined what caused Evan's stomach pain when he was first admitted to the hospital. Evan's and Pennys's lives were forever altered.

Blaine's devotion to his family and his son led to him co-founding MitoCanada, Canada's only not-for-profit organization focused on mitochondrial disease.

Personal bests

Half-marathon   1:12:38

Marathon   2:29:32

50Km   3:19:55

50 Miles   8:03:41

100Km   9:01:01

24 hours running   204 km

24 hours cross country skiing - 320 km

Knowing the story behind Blaine's running, I wanted to ask him a few questions about his record at the Toronto marathon.

What drove you to run as fast as you did dressed as a battery?

"The whole concept for running as a battery was to help raise awareness for mitochondrial disease by helping people make the simple connection that our mitochondria are the batteries of our cells. A Guinness World Record is an excellent way to get attention and media, so I thought by attempting the GWR for the 'Fastest marathon dressed as a battery' was a perfect

way to raise awareness for the cause and have a little fun at the same time."

"The costume was quite restrictive and awkward to run in to be honest, and very warm. We constructed it from sewing together three foam canvas laundry baskets (20" in diameter) and printing a fabric wrap with the Duracell rechargeable battery colours (copper and green) that provided the outside skin for the costume."

"Initially I was quite concerned about my ability to run a sub 4 hour marathon pace due to the restrictive nature of the costume. With a few tweaks and a couple 5k training runs, I felt it was possible. Once I got running in the race, it took me about 10k to find my efficient stride. The wind was very gusty throughout the race, which added to the difficulty factor. I went through the half in about 1:28 and realized a sub 3 hour was possible (and far exceeding my goal of 3:30). When things started to get tough towards the end, I thought about my son Evan and many others suffering from mitochondrial disease. I fed off their energy and the energy from those around me, to power myself to the line with everything I had in me achieving a time of 2:59:58 with just 2 seconds to spare."

What was the experience like and what was the reaction of other runners?

"It was really interesting seeing the reaction from the other runners. I started right at the back of the first (red) wave behind the 3:30 pacer as I didn't want to be obnoxious and

slow people down. Once I got running, I started slowly moving my way up through the field and was passing tons of people. Initially, I sensed people were thinking there's no way that battery guy can hold a 4:15/km pace in that costume and is going to run out of juice and explode on the course. Several people's responses were like "Seriously, a battery is passing me! But hey, dude that is a great cause and an incredible thing you are doing. Very inspiring, go for it!". I kept apologizing to people for passing and told them I was providing the best draft out on the course and to tuck in behind me."

"Some of my favourite parts of the run was listening to the fans shouting things like "Go battery man".... "Hey, it's the Duracell battery guy"..."I saw you on the news, great story keep running!" ...or "The Energizer Bunny is just up the road and is running out of energy needing a charge". Overall, it was an incredibly fun and enjoyable running experience."

What is it about running and raising awareness - so often running and raising awareness go together - your thoughts?

"I think it's a great way to be creative and rally a community for causes. I believe all runners aspire to run for a greater purpose than the individual pursuit, and running for charity/cause they connect with provides that for people. You can then take that to a whole other level when you attempt crazy, wacky, GWR's that are a spectacle and create life-long memories and friendships by running together as a team. Additionally, exercise is one of the best forms of therapies for people with mitochondrial disease for those who are able to tolerate it. Unfortunately for some people like Evan who are not able to exercise or run, Team Mito is out there inspired on their behalf to help make a difference under the slogan "Running for those who can't"."

How do you find time to train and be the CEO of MitoCanada?

"I approach exercise/training just like I approach other necessities in life, such as eating and sleeping, by thinking of it as essential for my day to day health to survive. With a busy family and work life, I need to plan ahead and put it in my schedule. I am extremely conscious of time and try to be efficient as possible. I mostly run, ride or ski from my doorstep and spend very little time driving to train. I guess ultimately, it's one of the highest priorities in my life and I just make the time for it."

What keeps you running and motivated as a busy dad and leader?

"I use a macro level goal of 1 hour of purposeful exercise a day on average through the year as my main guiding principle for health and training. I know myself well and that I am much more productive, happy and motivated when I run regularly. My wife Sarah is a runner as well and we travel to races together and find this an excellent way to experience new places. We also have a 12-year-old daughter (Julia), and we both feel it is important to be role models for her instilling the value and importance of life-long health. Aside from that,

I run with an amazing group of people here in Calgary called the 'Bow Valley Harriers' where I have developed a lot of great friends. It has become a big part of my social life and we keep each other motivated and challenged as we train together. We joke that our lifelong goal as a running group is to still be running together in our 80's and smiling like our good octogenarian friend Gerry Miller."

Blaine is an example of someone who has fond a passion for running but also found a reason to run.

There is struggle in life and running. It is how we handle it and how we come out of it that matters. Sometimes it's an easy battle to win, sometimes it a gut-wrenching, mind-tearing fight to come out from a dark place.

"What does not destroy me, makes me strong." – Nietzsche

Talking Running

Talking with Suzy

"We all have stories to tell and we all struggle at some point with life and running."

As I personally struggle mentally to motivate myself after my marriage broke up and dealing with being a single dad (and all that that brings)(my blog piece) – it is timely to talk with another runner who has battled on and off the track.

I am honoured to have had the chance to talk to Suzy Favor Hamilton who blistered many a track and was an elite level runner for many years. My Editors at the magazine I write a blog for (in addition to this one) did not bite and thought they had talked about Suzy enough as it was. They have their opinion but I wanted to profile Suzy. After reading her brave and brutally honest book 'Fast Girl' about her struggle with mental health and addictions that lead her eventually to Vegas, sex for money and the edge – I wanted to talk with her.

There was something in her story that touched me.

Suzy

US Junior Record Holder 1500m

3 National Junior Titles in High School

Scholastic Sports Magazine as one of the top 100 High School Athletes of the Century

Inducted into the US National High School Sports Hall of Fame in 2010

Nine NCAA Titles and 32 Big-Ten Championships

Won the Honda Cup and Babe Zaharias Awards for Top Female Collegiate Athlete in the US

Seven USA National titles

Two American Records

Three-time Olympian

Ran her specialty 1500m under 4:00 five times

Personal Bests

800m – 1:58.10 (2000)

1000m – 2:33.93 (1995)

1500m – 3:57.40 (2000)

Mile – 4:22.93 (1998)

3000m 8:46.16 (2000)

5,000m – 15:06.48 (2000)

Suzy loved to run as a young girl and also being competitive she started competing at something she loved. Although always torn between loving running and the stress of racing she excelled and eventually made it to the international level.

Like myself I was able to understand how a love of running and being competitive does not always mean one likes racing and the stress and pressure that comes with it. I love to run and run fast but sometimes, before and during a race I have struggled and not enjoyed the experience. I have had a few races where I was fit enough and the conditions perfect where I somehow had the mindset and environment to enjoy the experience and run a good time.

Suzy eventually found out she had bipolar disorder. I struggled with a temper when young, low self-esteem, confidence and still now occasionally depression. I managed in my own way but Suzy exacerbated by the wrong medication was sent her spiraling out of control. For more about her life you really should read her book.

I remember as a young runner seeing her on the cover of Runner's World and wanted to talk with her. I had the chance to ask her a few questions.

What was the highlight of your running career?

"That's a tough one. Making 3 Olympic teams comes to mind. Setting a couple American Records. My ninth NCAA Championship. But I think the one that brought me the most satisfaction was my victory in Oslo in 2000 when I ran 3:57.40 (1500m). I never thought I could go that fast, and I literally felt like I was flying at the end of that race."

What part does running play in your life now and can you now find joy in it?

"I recently blogged about this, so this is fresh in my mind. During my competitive career, as time went on, running became a chore for me. I internally felt I was running for the happiness of others as opposed to myself. The pure joy of running I had when I started out way back as a child was long gone. Professional track in particular had that effect on me. The anxiety I often experienced when it came to racing, the politics and corruption I saw and experienced first hand, the uneven playing field we compete on. It all took it's toll on me mentally and I wanted out. Never had the ability to use my voice to say so. But today, I believe through my difficult times post running career and now my recovery, I've been

able to separate all the crap from just plain running. I've realized how much I needed running to keep my brain relatively stable. It's taken me time to realize this, but today, I need running. My mind needs running. Back to that pure joy I had way back when. I'm recapturing that. My 48 year old legs put limits on my running, but I think that's not a bad thing. Slows things down for me. Allows me to focus on the enjoyment of it all."

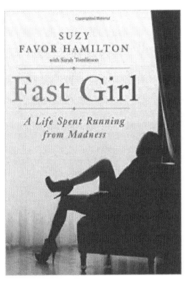

After your struggles, the book and *time- how are you doing now?*

"Relatively speaking, I'm good. I have many more good days than bad. During my depressive periods, I tend to withdraw and am best off being left alone, resting. These can last hours or days. They can still be very challenging both for myself, and for those closest to me, but we've all learned to better manage these times. But that being said, I would go so far as to say my life is the best it's ever been. Finally being properly diagnosed & medicated has had a lot to do with that. I now have clarity on so many things, I know how to better manage my illness, and have great support from my inner circle. So I can't complain about a thing really. I feel blessed in many ways."

Talking Running

After all these years what has running taught you about yourself?

"Ha, running has taught me toughness. Perseverance. All those killer training sessions in the Wisconsin winters. All the pretty dramatic trials and tribulations I experienced and all the physical pain from training and injuries. I believe that prepared me to make it through my world falling apart and through all the darkness I have experienced in recovery. I'll be forever grateful to my running for that."

What advice would you give someone some who has bipolar disorder?

"On social media, interviews and speeches, I try to emphasize two things. First, to get out there. I have found that exercise and just plain sometimes forcing yourself outside, out of bed, even if it means just walking around the block is so helpful for our illness. I believe running kept me relatively stable for many years. But motivation is the tough part during depressive periods. It's such a challenge to get yourself going. So I try to encourage the strength to get out there, despite the brain pushing back in such a big way. Second, that bipolar disorder is not a death sentence. One with bipolar disorder can live well with accurate diagnosis, quality therapy, proper meds, identification and reduction of life triggers and a support system. It's a challenging illness to say the least, but one that can be better handled by those living with it if society comes to understand it and no stigmatize it. Stigma prevents people from seeking help. That needs to change and it's a big reason I'm so vocal."

Talking Running

Suzy is now speaking out about her life and struggles and is a mental health advocate. Like many of us she also she still struggles with life and running. Life is about battle and the key is to moving forward.

Find Suzy on Twitter at @favorhamilton or her website/blog.

Find Suzy's book Fast Girl online.

Fast Girl:
Paperback: 304 pages
Publisher: Dey Street Books; Reprint edition (June 7, 2016)
Language: English
ISBN-10: 0062346202
ISBN-13: 978-0062346209

Run on Suzy.

This was published on my personal blog in January 2017.

Suzy is still an advocate for mental health, is active on social media and has her own blog, she continues as a motivational speaker and life coach. In a quick note this fall (2018) she said she was doing quite a bit of speaking and life coaching and focusing on mental health with a sex-positive slant.

Being a runner and a dad or mom is not a simple task. Parenting is a full time job on top of what most people do full-time to earn a living. Combine all that and it takes dedication, patience and flexibility.

"If you want to run, then run a mile. If you want to experience another life, run a marathon." – Emil Zatopek

Talking with another Running Dad

Love talking with other runners – and now its great to meet other running dads!

I am all over social media (mainly Twitter) and meet a lot of great runners. I like chatting and profiling a few now and then – everyone has a story to tell. Once in a while I get asked to share....like when I bumped into Denny and he invited me to be on his podcast DizRuns.

Meet the runner behind the microphone.

Denny Krahe

This American runner, dad and podcaster grew up in a small town in Northern Michigan and later moved to Florida for college and pretty much stayed there after. Denny this May will have been married for 11-years and like myself has a young 2 year-old daughter who he says keeps him on his toes.

Denny's real job is as a podcast host and running coach. He went to school to become an Athletic Trainer and worked as one for 10 years but took a risk and started his own business as a personal trainer. He now has a few face to face clients but is now focusing his efforts online to reach many more people and athletes.

And Denny was not always a runner: "I used to hate running. And I mean HATE! I grew up playing a variety of team sports, and running was always something you either did to get in shape for the season or as a punishment for screwing up at some point. I joked with my friends in high school that ran track that their sport was the worst possible sport in the world."

But something about running drew him back and he continued to try running. Working as a personal trainer at Middle Tennessee University with the track and cross country team he was drawn into running again. He started getting some miles in, and not long after actually stated enjoying lacing up and pounding the road. In 2010 he ran his first marathon (Walt Disney World) – and as many do, swore to never do another, then ran the same race the next year! He was hooked.

Dennny's running

5k: 19:54

10k: 44:58

13.1: 1:45:04

Talking Running

26.2: 4:08:34

Ultra: Successfully ran his first last week (March 2017)!

A chat with DizRuns: Listen to Denny's podcast chat with this skinny running dad! (http://www.dizruns.com/noel-paine/)

So why did you start your running podcast?

"I started my running show after doing a solo podcast for about 4 months in the health and fitness niche. I was enjoying podcasting, but doing a 20+ minute solo show was A LOT of work! I, naively, thought that doing a show with interviews

would be much less work and I was really getting into my running and the online running community at the time, so it seemed like a natural fit that my new show would be running based. I started reaching out to runners on Twitter, and got to work."

"The thing I enjoy most is connecting with other runners, both those that are on the show and those that I've built a relationship with online because they listen to the show. I'm not naturally the most talkative person, but there is something about connecting with folks that share a passion with me that makes all of my hesitancy to carry on a conversation go right out the window. While I'm running with someone, I feel like I could talk to them all day. Doing the podcast allows me to do that with people from around the world, which is pretty cool."

What was the funniest interview you have done?

"The most fun interview, eh? That's such a loaded question! I've probably had close to 250 interviews on the show now, so picking out one, or even ten, is next to impossible. There have been a handful, and I can't remember the folks off the top of my head, where I went into the interview without knowing much about the person at all beyond what information was in their twitter profile. No website to glean from. Google didn't help. And in each of those cases, once we get going the conversation takes on a life of it's own and that is always really cool to see happen."

"There have also been some fun ones where the conversation goes so far off the rails that I'm sure no one made it to the finish of the episode! Amy Marxhors and I talked about hockey and the 7 game series back in the 90s when my Red Wings beat her Blues when Steve Yzerman scored in double overtime on a shot from just outside the blue line. When I talked to Amelia Boone, we went off on a tangent about some different aspects of WWE and Wrestlemania."

"I think I just love the fact that I don't know where the conversations will always go, and it's fun to just let the show play out over the course of 45 minutes or so whether I'm talking to an Olympian or someone that is brand new to the sport."

Do you have a list of runners you'd like to have on your show?

"I really don't have a big list of people I'd love to have on the show. I kind of take it as it comes, and I love talking with "regular" runners as much as I enjoy talking with elites or celebs."

"That said, when I started the show I said I'd really like to talk to the two Peters: Shankman and Sagal. I had the chance to talk with Peter Shankman awhile back which was fun, but Peter Sagal has avoided me to this point. But someday, I'd like to talk with him."

What are your running goals for 2017?

"This year I'll be running my first ultra, which I'm somewhat surprised how excited I am for that experience. I'd also love to break 4 hours in the marathon, though I currently don't have any marathons I'm signed up for. I want to speak at 3-5 races, so I'm trying to keep my race schedule open so I'm flexible regarding speaking opportunities. And as a coach, I have a goal of 25+ PRs for my runners."

"My other big goal is to simply stay healthy. I've got a pretty good streak of no major injuries going, and I'm really dedicating myself this year to cross training as a way to improve my fitness while simultaneously helping to reduce the risk of injuries. So far so good on that front!"

I loved chatting with Denny on his show and loved chance to profile him. Meeting other runners and connecting is something I really enjoy. Check out Denny and his podcasts and tell him Noel sent ya!

Find Denny on Twitter @DizRuns

Find him on his webpage: http://www.dizruns.com/

This was published on my personal blog in March 2017.

Running can sometimes be a way to find yourself. Away from the noise of the world, with you only your thoughts and the sound of your feet on pavement of trail life seems more real.

I often feel most myself when laced up with feet on the ground.

"God has given me the ability. The rest is up to me. Believe. Believe. Believe." – Billy Mills

Son of famous drummer shows talent for steeplechase

Meet Aric Van Halen. This son of Van Halen drummer, Alex Van Halen, didn't inherit his dad's talent for music. Instead, he shines on the track.

Aric Van Halen is 26, from Los Angeles and is the son of Van Halen drummer Alex Van Halen.

That he's the son of a well-known drummer is intriguing but what's also impressive is his running ability.

Starting to run during his freshman year of high school, Aric caught the attention of the gym teacher after running a 6:05 mile for a fitness test. The coach suggested Aric come out for the cross-country team.

His potential talent turned into real ability. With some training, he became the school's top runner by the end of the season. In the spring he had to decide whether or not he's run track or go for the baseball team.

Talking Running

"I decided to try out for the baseball team and halfway through tryouts I realized the love of the game wasn't there anymore. So I informed the baseball coach at the end of the day that I wouldn't be back the next day and I would be doing track. Twelve years later I'm still running track," he says.

The running continued after he left that school and headed to the University of Colorado. The lanky blonde runner with a talent for the steeplechase ran his best time in the event while running against Canadian Olympian Taylor Milne.

Aric Van Halen's PBs

800m	1:52.54
1500m	3:44.42
Mile	4:03.52
3,000m	7:53.74 (indoors)
3,000m steeplechase	8:32.92
5,000m	14:01.54

I got chance to ask Aric a few questions:

What are your race and running goals for 2016?

I'm not 100 per cent sure yet. I'm still trying to get fit and ready for the U.S. Olympic Trials. But I'll probably do Payton Jordan, hopefully Oxy High Performance and maybe do a 1,500 somewhere between then and the Trials, and then hopefully do the Trials. I don't currently have a standard since I missed all of last season with an injury but I'm fairly confident I can get to 8:30 shape by May. My goal this season is to PR, in everything, and a top 5 finish at the Olympic Trials.

Does attention from your family name ever distract from running or other goals?

I don't really find it a distraction. I get asked about it a lot, "Oh sweet last name are you related?" Stuff like that and depending on the situation or the mood I'll say yes or no. It happens at the airport a lot of the time, when they're looking at my ticket and ID. One ticket lady even sang Panama to me while she printed out my ticket because I was her "captive audience." But all in all, people who know me know I don't talk about it much and I can get a little uncomfortable when asked about it.

What motivates you to run and push yourself?

My motivation to run and push myself is a combination of passion for the sport and an intense competitiveness. I like running a lot, especially when you're healthy and fit, but what I LOVE is racing. People can argue PRs and tactics and race situations all they want, but when it comes down to it, racing is pure: the gun goes off and the first person to cross the line is the winner and there are very few things like the rush of coming around the last turn, in what feels like full sprint, going for the win.

Aric is currently a photographer and cameraman and running after his dreams of running even faster.

This article was originally published in Canadian Running magazine in February 2016.

Aric continues to run but not at the same level, but still enjoys jumping into the occasional race.

We are all limited by the genes we are given and a set Vo2max. How fast we are is often defined by who is around us and who shows up on race day. If we are not going to be in the Olympics or set a world record we must all find our own goals, our reason to run and what will make us happy.

"The essential thing in life is not so much conquering as fighting well." – Baron de Coubertin

Kenyan Runningdad

Talking with marathoner Justin Lagat

"We all have fathers and runners are no different."

It is a mild but overcast spring evening and my legs have 25-kilometres of running on them. I am typing away with a cup of Kenyan tea in a mug beside me and my Kenyan friend Justin Lagat is glued to a replay of last year's Ottawa marathon. Its a good day.

Justin is in town (Ottawa) and crashing on my couch so he can run the Ottawa Sporting Life 10k as a warm-up for the Ottawa marathon at the end of May. I hung out with my fellow running dad and friend for the weekend. Here is a bit about Justin and a few things he had to say about running, training and being a running dad.

Justin Lagat

(Bio from Justin's profile for the Ottawa marathon, where he is an ambassador) Justin grew up in the rural area of the Rift Valley region in Kenya. His primary school was about four kilometers away from home and as a kid he, with his siblings, would run to and from the school four times in a day making it a total of 16km daily. He believes this, in addition to his genes, made him grow into a runner.

However, in a land where everyone is born into the same life situations, it was hard for him to make a great impression as an exceptional runner in the region. He would only win in some low profile competitions, but that was enough to jump-start his career in running.

Running and writing, which is his other passion, have blended well and besides running he is also a columnist with RunBlogRun, author of Determined Runners (e-book)and a freelance sports journalist covering the sport of running. His work has been featured in a number of international media including the Competitor.com and Thrive Sports.

So far, he has completed three marathons, one being the 2016 Ottawa Marathon, during which he had to push on to the finish despite the heat. His aim from now on is to complete at least two marathons every year.

Justin's personal bests

10K 29:48

Half-marathon 1:06

I took a few moments to ask Justin a few questions:

How do you balance being an elite runner and being a dad, is it hard being away from your family?

"When you are leaving a young daughter (3-years old) it is hard to hear her ask when daddy will be home. When she was younger it was hard because she needed so much attention and I needed to be a dad – now she is going to school and I can train and rest after without any interruptions!"

If all goes well with your training and your taper – what would you like to run at the 2017 Ottawa marathon?

"My goal is to run under 2:10, to run as fast as I can. It would take things to the next level for me and I would hopefully get

more recognition, sponsorship and the ability to run at more international-caliber races."

North Americans always want to know the secret to the Kenyan running success, is it the barrels of tea, the training at altitude or just plain hard work in your opinion?

"I think it is the hard work and the motivation to do what it takes to succeed in running, in a country already filled now with fast runners – that have driven our success."

How do your rate my cheese and cucumber sandwiches?

"I give it a 6 out of 10....I prefer hot foods more." (I think he was being nice)

Sunday update: Justin ran the Ottawa Sportinglife 10k (which raises money for the local CHEO Hosptial). Justin loved the fact the race was flat, fast and raised money for a great cause. He also won the race in a time of 31:02!

*A big shout out to the friendly and great folks at InStride management (who manged the Ottawa race) who put on a great race and were super welcoming to Justin!

**A big thanks to Justin for being a cool guy and introducing me to Kenyan tea! (now addicted)

You can find Justin on his blog and on Twitter at @kenyanathlete

This was published on my persaonl blog in May 2017.

Justin continues to run and train and is aiming for a sub 2:20 marathon and more racing in North America.

The rush and joy of breaking the finish line tape at a race is a feeling I wish everyone had the chance to enjoy. Just finishing is an accomplishment, or achieving a personal best or goal can also but emotion, but to be first is unique.

"When you run the marathon, you run against the distance, not against the other runners and not against the time. " - Haile Gebrselassie

One of the quick ones

Ok so I am a little late with this...I meant to jump on this and have it up right after the 2017 Vancouver marathon. I did not happen. I had been watching the results of the Vancouver marathon earlier this year and saw a story about an almost unknown runner showing up as the top Canadian runner at the international calibre event. I was intrigued. I also noticed his last name – same as a co-worker in Ottawa.

Sometimes Canada is as small as we joke about it being – big land mass but very connected population. So one thing led to another and I connected with this runner –meet Michael.

Michael Trites

Michael is another east coaster like myself, being originally from Berwick, Nova Scotia, a small town in rural Nova Scotia (I remember running a race there years ago). Like many maritimers he moved away for studies in 2013 and is still in school pursuing a PhD in Physiology at the University of Alberta.

Michael Trites the top Canadian at the 2017 Vancouver Marathon

Michael however only started running when he started graduate school, running recreationally 3-4 times a week without any structured training program. He quickly discovered he was not half bad at it quickly after jumping into the Edmonton Half Marathon and running 1:25. The new runner became I hooked on the Alberta running community and even did a brief stint with the University of Alberta Golden Bears Cross-Country team. As he got more serious he found a coach and a club and now trains with the Edmonton-based Running Room Athletic Club (RRAC) coached by Matthew

Norminton. The RRAC has several athletes in Edmonton who race primarily middle- and long-distance events from 800 meters on the track to trail ultra-marathons, and everything in between.

I liked the Nova Scotia connection and always like chatting with runners. New enthusiasm and newness to the sport almost oozes out with the sweat on his forehead – and there is nothing wrong with that. Sometimes I miss the newness of running.

Michael is sponsored by the Running Room and below are some of his recent race performances.

2017 BMO Vancouver Marathon (2:34:07)

2017 Jasper Canadian Rockies Half-Marathon (1:16:16) 2nd

2017 Banff Marathon 10k road race (34:11) 1st and course record

2016 Mizuno Midsummer 5k (15:53) 5th

I tracked down Michael and asked him a few questions:

How did it feel to be top Canadian at the Vancouver marathon?

"It was an exciting surprise to be the top Canadian at the BMO Vancouver Marathon. There were a lot of outstanding Canadian athletes there at the race. I just tried to focus on the variables I could control (my race plan, efforts, pacing, etc.)

rather than variables outside of my control (other athletes race plans, placing, etc.). It was great to see the hours on the treadmill and running through the frigid Edmonton winter come to fruition."

What are your goals this year?

"My goal for this year is to dip under 2:30 in a fall marathon. Currently I don't have any other races on my calendar, however depending on how the build-up for the fall marathon progresses I may try and improve my half-marathon or 10k PB in a late summer race. However I may adapt this goal a few times depending on the time-constrains I end up facing with school."

What drives you to run and race?

"The main drive in getting me out to run and race is the Edmonton running community. I am quickly realizing how small (and passionate) it is. I have been incredibly fortunate to be able to meet inspiring people from diverse backgrounds that all share a thirst to run. I am not going to try and name everyone, because I am sure I would miss someone. However, even if they train with one of the other groups in Edmonton, whether it be the Running Room Athletic Club, Fast Trax, Run Collective, November project, RunLab, etc. Seeing everyone else out there and hearing the stories keeps me pounding the pavement."

Winning a race is always a thrill and something I wish everyone could experience, but we cannot – thus we often live through the victories of others and dream. Keep running Michael and hope you achieve your goals!

This article was written for my personal blog in 2016. Michael is still running and running well. In 2018 went back to the Vancouver marathon and ran 2:31:42, 2nd overall behind Olympian Rob Watson.

Cree Proverb

"Realize that we as human beings have been put on this earth for only a short time and that we must use this time to gain wisdom, knowledge, respect and the understanding for all human beings since we are all relatives."

"ka-kí-kiskéyihtétan óma, namoya kinwés maka aciyowés pohko óma óta ka-hayayak wasétam askihk, ékwa ka-kakwéy miskétan kiskéyihtamowin, iyinísiwin, kistéyitowin, mina nánisitotatowin kakiya ayisiniwak, ékosi óma kakiya ka-wahkotowak."

Talking Running

Running to beat my shadow

No one is ever prepared for the loss of a parent. Parents are supposed to be around until they are old and grey and even then, most of us are seldom prepared to lose them. Like running, we expect to get through a run without interruption, twists, turns or the occasional dog jumping out at you are not what you expect.

Life itself is an un-ending series of changes and unexpected events, whether we realize it or not. A few years ago, I found myself dragging myself out to run with a young aboriginal man who was doing a run he did to help raise awareness about murdered and missing aboriginal women in Canada. His name was Thealand Kicknosway, a proud Potawatami/ Cree Nation young man with an amazing positive energy and a desire to change the world. I connected with him, his mom and those who were out running and returned to find him the next year. This is how I met Vicky.

Vicky Laforge

You can feel the enthusiasm and motivation emanating from Vicky and you can see the excitement in her eyes. I did not see it the first time I met her but I certainly did when I got the chance to run with her. The first time I met Vicky I was told of how she was running for her parents and especially her mother who would have been celebrating her birthday that very day. Vicky was running for a reason. Only later, would she tell me her story and allow me to share it. It is a personal story of pain, mourning and transformation.

"My life changed one day. My parents died in a tragic way, in a double homicide. It is something that you can never prepare for. It is something that can never change. It is something that you can never forget. What do you do? How can you heal from it?"

Vicky's parents were sheltering her aunt in their cottage, who had just left an abusive relationship. Her aunt's ex-husband went and shot both her parents and then kidnapped her aunt. Vicky's aunt escaped but life would never be the same. She struggled to deal with the loss and the upheaval it brought to her life.

"Soon after the tragedy I put on a lot of weight, I felt weighed down with heavy emotions, but I continued with therapy and tried to relieve the pain I felt through my own ceremonial ways from my Ojibway culture, went to church, group therapy, prayer, being an advocate. I spoke out about  violence against women, since this is the reason for their murders. I worked with victims services in a committee as a victim, spoke to numerous groups about our family experience and promoted the use of women's shelters. I struggled and perhaps all of these ways were good and brought me to a place of healing, but I know that I rarely felt myself.

"Around the time of the hearings for the murder, I took up kickboxing. It was approaching two years after their murders when I began classes. I was hooked and was getting fit and felt strong. But the best reason for taking up kickboxing was to feel like I could fight back. I have so many nightmares and in my dreams, I would turn around and start fighting. My

Talking Running

*physical abilities gave me power and strength. I eventually
fell off the kickboxing wagon when I moved to a new city. I
loved it and regretted leaving that club."*

Without an outlet and with the memories and trauma
still fresh, Vicky fell into depression and felt like she did not
have any personal power.

*"I would often feel vulnerable and incapable of keeping my
life in order because I would be on a rollercoaster of emotions
every year."*

*"I eventually got up to weight of 295 pounds and my weight
made me feel even more depressed and vulnerable. You could
physically see my unhappiness in life. You could see that I
was exploding inside and it took on a physical form on my
body. Many people do not know my struggles and I wanted
so badly to change and have more in life. I wanted to have my
strength and power back. The death I felt inside of my heart
and body was and is painful to carry."*

Running for her life

Vicky decided she wanted to make changes and fight for her
life. Inspired by a friend who was also battling weight she went
to a doctor to see about a gastric bypass. She wanted change.

*"When I was young teenager, I was super athletic and I was a
very physical girl. My greatest regret in life was that I did not
take better care of my body and stay fit. I imagined what my
life would be like if I ever got a second chance in life. I would
see myself running like I did in high school. When I was a kid,*

my brother would say that I would run and try to beat my shadow all of the time. He would come to my races when I was a teenager. I once ran in Toronto at High Park for a cross-country running race. It was amazing having him cheering me on."

Then she found out it would be a long wait before she was allowed to have gastric bypass surgery. Vicky slid back into depression, became bulimic and hated herself. She wanted her second chance. But like before she was down but not defeated. She decided to change things up and began going to the gym and taking spinning classes. She would also find running shoes and try a run occasionally but found it was too hard on her knees. But she kept working out. Eventually the day of the operation arrived and then she jumped right back into working out after.

"I was terrified of loose skin on my arms and body so I decided I would work out as much as i could. This slowed my weight loss because I actually had to eat more. A year into my new physical healing journey I went to a workshop at the Ottawa Triathlon Club. I wanted to learn about everything to do with triathlons. I could see on their videos that even larger people would take part. I thought maybe I can do this. I ended up on their mailing list and got an invite for joining the club and I began with the swimming in September 2017."

From swimming, Vicky moved on to tackling cycling months later in January. She started indoors with spinning classes and dreamed about triathlons. She had two disciplines down and one to go.

Talking Running

"I became inspired by all of the other participants and wanted to be just like them. Listening to their triathlon adventures and training sessions. I was training longer and harder than most, but I couldn't run. I wanted to achieve this goal. I was losing weight, getting fit and had my second chance in life and wanted a goal to achieve to show my new skill and change in my body. I decided to ask the doctor about options for my knees and he sent me to physiotherapy. I was there for four months until my coverage ran out from work to pay for the sessions. I continued to lose weight and the doctor said to try running when I hit 150lbs. That was depressing because I really wanted to start but was still 190lbs. I was training so much and wanted to get to it. Someone told me that a racer actually walked the running portion of the ironman and made it in time to complete the race. I was shocked and thought yes, I can do this. My dreams will come true. So I went to the gym and got on the treadmill."

She found working incredibly boring but kept at it. One day at a slow pace, she decided to throw in a jog. She tried five minutes of running and then five of walking.

"It was a very slow pace and I am not sure the distance it was, but I was really excited that i was jogging. All of the physiotherapy really strengthened my knee and I felt pain and iced afterwards but it was a start. I eventually jogged 30 minutes straight and my first outdoor run was on a cold spring evening. The ground had ice patches but I managed to jog 4 km."

Where many would give in, Vicky kept pushing herself and stayed motivated.

"The Ottawa triathlon Club they would do 2 hours on the bike and then 20 minutes of running. I went out and did my best. I jogged very slowly and it was winter but I did it. I didn't care that I was the slowest one. I even saw people walking and they were walking faster than my jog at times. I kept going. I did strength training, the club coaches showed me appropriate

stretches, and I worked out hard every week. My family commented that they had never seen me so determined. I said this is my second chance, I'd always dreamed of this and that I did not want to blow it."

Vicky did her first triathlon in June of 2018. After two years of training and an operation, her day had arrived to swim, bike and run.

"The day was the most exhilarating experience of my life. My

brother was there for me, just like when we were kids. We held each other at the end of the race and cried. He asked me often why I was so hard on myself. I just listened and never explained. But I think that day he felt my joy and he has never asked me again why I do what I do to stay fit."

"I physically removed the pain from my body. I still have pain within but I am dealing with it differently. I swim bike and run to ease my pain and it helps me to feel life and my own power. I worked up to a 10km run with the Canadian Army Run this past September. I literally ran 10km two weeks before the race. It was so hard on my body but I didn't care. I

Talking Running

used ice, protein, massage and prayer. I ran the 10km in one hour and thirty minutes. Which was my fastest run by ten minutes."

"Running and exercise is saving my life. There is no turning back for this girl. I am fit, healthy and I weigh 127 lbs less. I am a different woman!"

Vicky continues to run, bike and swim and is looking for new challenges and continuing her journey of healing and growth. Her shadow now has a hard time keeping up with her.

Vicky Laforge, her daughter and their dog call Winnipeg home now and if you see her, she will most likely be moving.

Sometimes life and running have unexpected turns and twists and the path you started on leads you somewhere unexpected. Sometimes you can even find and see new things on a path you have been on before, when you are in a different frame of mind.

Talking Running

"Sometimes it is the journey not the destination that counts in running. Make sure you enjoy your time on foot." – Noel Paine

The Reason I run

It is more the adventure and the process I enjoy than the destination.

It was 5am in the morning and I was standing at the edge of a canyon and not able to see much further than the length of my arm. I was far from home, shivering and anxious as I stood at the rim of the Grand Canyon. It was bigger and more awe-inspiring than I could have imagined. I had arrived the day before to prepare for my run across the Canyon and back and been floored. If you could hear jaws drop then you would have heard mine crack the rocky edge of that immense canyon the afternoon I arrived. It was so much bigger, wider and deeper than any photo can portray. The books and videos had done nothing to prepare me.

I was at the start of a running adventure. It was not a race and no one had forced me to the steep, dark and winding path that led down the Grand Canyon wall. I was there because I loved to run. I had wanted a challenge, had wanted something I could do on foot to help me battle some inner demons and some issues in my life at the time. The Grand Canyon had also looked like an insanely beautiful place to visit, if not run.

It was going to be a long run and one that held many unknowns - as a runner who had never been to the Canyon before. I had researched, read books, watched videos and been training hard and had recently classed myself as a sort of ultra-capable runner after doing a few ultra-trail runs (100km).

The experience and research did nothing to help unclench my sphincter or settle my guts. I was nervous, fit and soon was descending slowly along a path that wound 7-miles

Talking Running

into the mile deep gorge cut through the rock by the Colorado River. Did I mention the sun had not yet risen?

Dodging the occasional pile of donkey poop that I spotted with the bobbing light of my headlamp I ran down the dusty path and stairs cut into the canyon wall. I ignored thinking about the few thousand-foot drop to one side of me. I focused on the task ahead and waited for the sunrise as I ran further.

The sun slowly rose from its hiding place below the horizon and started to light up the top of the canyon. Shadows started diving for cover and the amazing scene around me started to materialize. The colours of dirt and rock changed as I descended and I could hardly contain my joy and wonder at where I was running. Every turn offered another fantastic view or a cool, narrow path to run along.

I descended, legs pounded by the grueling descent and steep steps. It was then a run over bridges, along the biting cold and beautiful Colorado River with the thousands of feet of canyon looming over me on either side – also reminding me I eventually would have to run back up.

I was doing the infamous rim2rim2rim, around 65km of down, across, up, down, back across and up – depending on what route you chose. It was not a race but an epic bucket list for many trail and ultra runners. I was knee deep in the bucket and still running.

I made it across, then up narrow and winding trail along the north rim and then stopped for a few minutes, questioned my sanity and started the run back. I had a shuttle waiting for me and had guesstimated the time the run would take. Guess wrong and I would be sleeping on my bag at the edge of the canyon for the night. No time to doddle.

I took my time as in I was careful but ran quickly where I could and got back late afternoon. The trek up took all my will power and all I could think of on the way up was dreamy pictures of cold frosty coke bottles.

I let out a howl when I hit the top. It really sunk in; what I had accomplished and where I had run. I'd been alone on the trail for a long time on trails I'd never run. I'd had only my thoughts for company and the sound of my feet hitting the trail. There had been no bib numbers, no noisy runners around me. I had just been running for hours to explore – and because I liked to run. That's when I realized I really do like to run. Who knew.

About my running:

I am just an average runner who is a bit faster than the middle of the pack guys and gals once in a while. I started running at age 12 and have never really stopped. Blessed with a light frame and some speed I ran middle distance in high school and pretty much have run every track event (100m, 100 hurdles, 200m, 400m, 600m, 800m, 1000m, 3000m, 3000m steeplechase) and tried everything on the road with the exception of a few odd distances. After my first marathon

Personal bests:

800m	2:03
1500m	4:20
5k	16:14
10K	35:18
Marathon	2:54

I have run the Boston marathon, Grand Canyon (rim2rim2rim), a few 100-kilomtre trail ultramarathons and one 258-kilometre 2.5-day 40th birthday run along the Rideau Trail in Ottawa, Ontario (Canada). The above is in addition to an insane number of road races, track meets, relays and trail runs.

Noel Paine is a Canadian runner, writer, blogger and runningdad with a passion for running and healthy, active living. He has battled depression and some dark places in life but has battled back to anew positive path. Noel has been running for over 30-years and run everything from the 100m to 100km ultramarathons and across and back the Grand Canyon. He has written for Canadian Running magazine, iRun magazine and interviewed world record holders, Olympians and one Canadian Prime Minister among many.

Blog: https://nopainenogainblog.wordpress.com/

Twitter: @NoelPaine

Instagram: @runningwriter

Podcast: https://anchor.fm/noel-paine

Talking Running

Running Dad

Talking Running

Made in the USA
Columbia, SC
23 October 2020